Key Stage
BITESIZE
revision

Check and test

Science

**Morton Jenkins, Rod Clough,
Mary Whitehouse**

Published by BBC Educational Publishing,
BBC White City, 201 Wood Lane, London W12 7TS.

First published 2003. Reprinted March 2004.

© Morton Jenkins, Rod Clough, Mary Whitehouse / BBC Worldwide (Educational Publishing), 2001.
All rights reserved.

ISBN 0 563 54357 4

Illustrations by Hardlines Ltd
Index complied by Indexing Specialists
Reproduced by Spectrum Colour, England
Printed in Italy by Poligrafico Dehoniano

Contents

About the KS3 Bitesize service

KS3 Bitesize is a revision service designed to help you achieve success in the National Tests. There are books, television programmes and a website, which can be found at **www.bbc.co.uk/education/revision**. It's called *Bitesize* because it breaks revision into bite-sized chunks to make it easier to learn. *Check and Test* is the latest addition to the *Bitesize* revision service.

How to use this book

This book is divided into the 100 essential things you need to know, so your revision is quick and simple. It provides a quick test for each bite-sized chunk so you can check that you know it!

Use this book to check your understanding of KS3 Science.
If you can prove to yourself that you're confident with these key ideas, you'll know that you're on track with your learning.

You can use this book to test yourself:
- during your KS3 course
- at the end of the course during revision.

As you revise, you can use *Check and Test* in several ways:
- as a summary of the essential information on each of the 100 topics to help you revise those areas
- to check your revision progress: test yourself to see how confident which you are with each topic
- to keep track and plan your time: you can aim to check and test a set number of topics each time you revise, knowing how many you need to cover in total and how much time you've got.

More KS3 Bitesize resources

Key Stage 3 Bitesize Revision: Science is a book that contains the key information and skills you need to revise, plus lots of tips and practice questions to help you improve your results. ISBN: 0 563 47433 5

The KS3 Bitesize Revision: Science website provides even more practice and explanation to help you revise. It can be found at **www.bbc.co.uk/education/revision**.

Topic checker

Use the topic checkers on this page to keep track of the topics you've covered as you work through them. They're also useful to double-check that you've covered each area.

- Once you're confident with a topic and can answer the questions, you can cross the topic number off the first grid. As you check the topic for a second or third time, you can cross it off each grid.

- You'll be able to see which topics you've covered most thoroughly and those which you haven't done as much work on. Is this because you're confident that you know these topics or are you putting off looking at them?

- Any problem topics should sink in by your third check.

- Don't worry if you don't have time to go over each topic three times. Every time you look at a topic, you'll be able to remember a little bit more.

First time

1	2	3	4	5	6	7	8	9	10
11	12	13	14	15	16	17	18	19	20
21	22	23	24	25	26	27	28	29	30
31	32	33	34	35	36	37	38	39	40
41	42	43	44	45	46	47	48	49	50
51	52	53	54	55	56	57	58	59	60
61	62	63	64	65	66	67	68	69	70
71	72	73	74	75	76	77	78	79	80
81	82	83	84	85	86	87	88	89	90
91	92	93	94	95	96	97	98	99	100

Second time

1	2	3	4	5	6	7	8	9	10
11	12	13	14	15	16	17	18	19	20
21	22	23	24	25	26	27	28	29	30
31	32	33	34	35	36	37	38	39	40
41	42	43	44	45	46	47	48	49	50
51	52	53	54	55	56	57	58	59	60
61	62	63	64	65	66	67	68	69	70
71	72	73	74	75	76	77	78	79	80
81	82	83	84	85	86	87	88	89	90
91	92	93	94	95	96	97	98	99	100

Third time

1	2	3	4	5	6	7	8	9	10
11	12	13	14	15	16	17	18	19	20
21	22	23	24	25	26	27	28	29	30
31	32	33	34	35	36	37	38	39	40
41	42	43	44	45	46	47	48	49	50
51	52	53	54	55	56	57	58	59	60
61	62	63	64	65	66	67	68	69	70
71	72	73	74	75	76	77	78	79	80
81	82	83	84	85	86	87	88	89	90
91	92	93	94	95	96	97	98	99	100

BBC KS3 Check and Test: Science

Check the facts

All plants and animals are made up of building blocks called cells.

Animal cells never contain **chloroplasts** or **cell walls** but they all have **cytoplasm** and **cell membranes**.

Nearly all living animal cells have a **nucleus**.

All living plant cells contain cytoplasm, a nucleus, a cell membrane, and a cell wall.

Those plant cells which grow in light often have chloroplasts.

Plant cell walls contain **cellulose** and many plant cells have bubble-like **vacuoles** inside them. These vacuoles contain a liquid called **cell sap**.

Test yourself

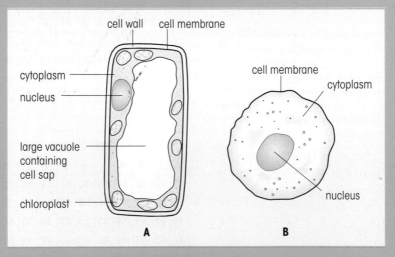

cell wall   cell membrane

cytoplasm

nucleus

large vacuole
containing
cell sap

chloroplast

A

cell membrane

cytoplasm

nucleus

B

1 Which part of cell A is made of cellulose? *Plant cell walls*

2 Give three reasons for calling cell B an animal cell. *It doesn't have cell walls, large vacuole & chloroplast*

3 Name three parts that are the same in plant cells and in animal cells. *Nucleus, cytoplasm, cell membrane*

4 How do potato cells, growing underground, differ from those in a leaf?
Potato cells would not need chloroplasts to trap the sunlight.

Check the facts

Vacuoles contain a watery liquid called **cell sap**, which pushes on the outer parts of the cell, keeping the cell turgid (firm).

The **cell membrane** is made up of **protein** and **fat**. The membrane controls what moves in and out of the cell.

The **nucleus** contains the instructions for running the cell. There is a **nuclear membrane** surrounding it.

The plant **cell wall** is a firm layer that holds plants together and gives them much of their strength to support themselves.

Chloroplasts contain a green substance, called **chlorophyll**, which absorbs energy from sunlight and helps plants to make food.

The **cytoplasm** is where most chemical reactions take place. For example, it is where **sugar** is used to release energy and where proteins are made.

Test yourself

1 Which part of the cell could be described as its control centre?

2 What would a plant cell be unable to do if it did not have chloroplasts?

3 Describe what you would expect to happen to a plant if it lost water from its vacuoles.

4 Which part of an animal cell, besides the cytoplasm, has a membrane surrounding it?

5 Where in a cell would you find cell sap?

Check the facts

Organisms are made up of different **cells**, which have special jobs.

Nerve cells carry messages in the form of electrical energy.

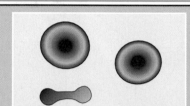

nucleus

cytoplasm

Red blood cells carry oxygen.

Muscle cells contract and relax, as bundles of long cells or as flat sheets, which surround parts of the body.

cytoplasm   nucleus

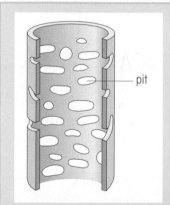

pit

Plants have some cells that are hollow and long. They have firm **cell walls**, made of a woody substance, called **lignin**. They are called **xylem** (pronounced z-eye-lem) **cells**. These act like drainpipes to carry water and **minerals** from the roots to the leaves.

Plants also have some cells for storing food, such as **starch**.

Test yourself

1 Match the type of cell in the list below to the activity it helps.

Cells		Activity	
1	Nerve	**A**	Movement
2	Muscle	**B**	Carrying oxygen
3	Red blood cell	**C**	Carrying water
4	Xylem	**D**	Sensitivity

Check the facts

Food is our fuel and gives us energy so we can move and grow.

The classes of food which help us move and grow are:

Carbohydrates	Fats	Proteins
Carbohydrates include **sugars** and **starch** and are the main providers of energy. Cereals and potatoes are rich sources of carbohydrates.	Fats can release energy and can be stored in our bodies. Rich sources are butter, lard and margarine.	Proteins provide materials for growth and repair. Rich sources are meat, fish, wheat and beans.

To help carry out important chemical reactions in our bodies the following chemicals are needed:

Vitamins	Minerals
Rich sources of vitamin C are fresh fruit and vegetables. Vitamins A and D are found in liver and dairy products.	Most minerals are found in fruits and vegetables, but a rich source of **calcium** is milk and a rich source of iron is meat, particularly liver.

Test yourself

1 Which class of food provides materials for bodybuilding? Name two foods that are rich in this class.

2 Which class of food is easy to store in the body as an energy reserve?

3 In a chicken sandwich what is the main class of food in:
   a) the bread   b) the chicken   c) the butter?

4 Why can food be described as our fuel?

5 Explain why milk may be described as an all-purpose food.

Humans as organisms

Check the facts

A balanced diet is essential to remain healthy. If you do not have a balanced diet, you will suffer from malnutrition (you can be over-weight and still suffer from malnutrition).

On average, a balanced diet should consist of:

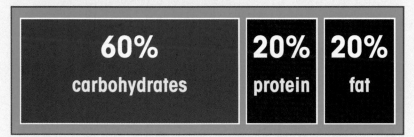

| **60%** carbohydrates | **20%** protein | **20%** fat |

Besides carbohydrate, protein and fat, we also need very small amounts of **vitamins** and **minerals** to help with our bodies' chemistry. The total amount of these needed every day may be only a tiny fraction of a gram.

Without enough of the proper vitamins and minerals we can suffer from conditions called **deficiency diseases**. **Scurvy** is caused by not having enough **vitamin C** and **anaemia** is caused by not having enough **iron**.

Test yourself

1 What class of food might be the cause of malnutrition by making you overweight?

2 Why might a person with a job involving a lot of muscular effort need more than 60% carbohydrate in their diet?

3 Explain why sailors who went on long voyages of discovery in the 18th Century suffered from scurvy.

4 What is the difference between the terms 'starvation' and 'malnutrition'?

Check the facts

Digestion is the breakdown of large, insoluble particles of food into small, soluble particles so that they can pass into the blood system and be carried all around the body.

The breakdown of food begins with **mechanical digestion** in the mouth. Here, chewing takes place to break the food down so that it can be mixed with **saliva** and swallowed.

digestive enzymes After chewing, **chemical digestion** begins to break down large, insoluble molecules into small, soluble molecules. This takes place with chemicals called **digestive enzymes**. *digestive enzymes*

Enzymes

- An **enzyme** is a **protein** made by the body to speed up the rate of chemical reactions.

- Most enzymes have nothing to do with digestion. Just one small group of enzymes help to digest food.

- Each class of food has its own type of enzyme to help break it down.

Test yourself

1 What happens to food when it is digested?

2 Why does food have to be digested?

3 Name the type of protein used to break down food?

4 What is used in chemical digestion that is not used in mechanical digestion?

5 In humans, where does mechanical digestion and chemical digestion take place at the same time?

Humans as organisms

BBC KS3 Check and Test: Science

Humans as organisms

Check the facts

Human blood consists of a pale yellow, clear liquid, called plasma, which contains red blood cells and white blood cells and parts of broken-down cells, called platelets.

The liquid in a blister is plasma. It normally carries useful materials or solution to cells. Plasma also carries **waste materials** from the cells so that the cells will not be harmed by them.

The useful substances carried by the plasma include the products of **digestion**, such as **blood sugar** (**glucose**) and digested **proteins** and **fats**. It also carries **minerals**, **vitamins** and the chemical messengers of the body, called **hormones**.

Waste products carried by the plasma include **carbon dioxide** (combined with other chemicals) and **urea**, which is found in **urine**.

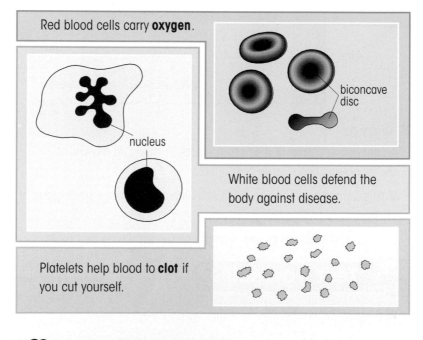

Red blood cells carry **oxygen**.

biconcave disc

nucleus

White blood cells defend the body against disease.

Platelets help blood to **clot** if you cut yourself.

Test yourself

1 Why are red blood cells important?

2 What useful materials does plasma carry to your cells?

3 How is blood used in getting rid of waste?

4 Give two ways in which blood protects you against disease.

Check the facts

The human **skeleton** is able to move because it has **joints**.

We could not move around without a skeleton. It allows movement because it forms a firm base for the attachment of **muscles**, which join the bone on either side of joints.

Two types of joints are important to us and are shown below. They are the **hinge joint**, found at our elbows and knees, and the **ball-and-socket joint** found at our shoulders and hips.

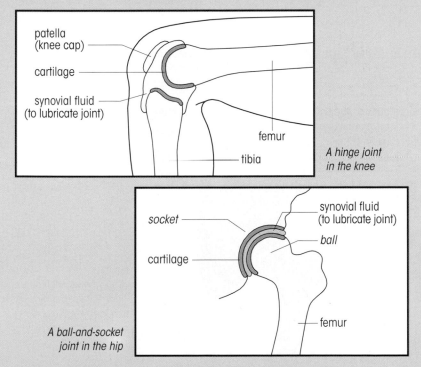

A hinge joint in the knee

A ball-and-socket joint in the hip

The skeleton protects the important delicate **organs** by surrounding them with a hard cage.

It supports the body because it is made of tough solid materials, which help animals to stand upright.

Test yourself

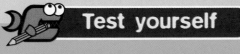

1 List the jobs carried out by your skeleton.

2 What features are needed by all skeletons for them to be able to move?

3 What is the difference between the way in which a ball-and-socket joint works and the way in which a hinge joint works?

Humans as organisms

Humans as organisms

Check the facts

Joints occur where bones meet. There is movement in most joints, caused by muscles.

After contracting, a muscle cannot lengthen itself again and has to be pulled back into shape. Muscles are often arranged in antagonistic pairs, with one pulling one way and the other pulling back, to overcome this problem.

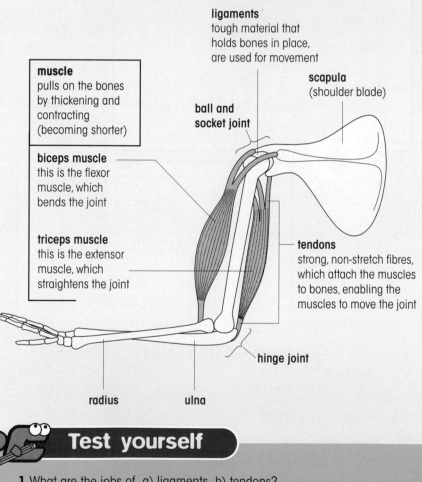

ligaments
tough material that holds bones in place, are used for movement

muscle
pulls on the bones by thickening and contracting (becoming shorter)

biceps muscle
this is the flexor muscle, which bends the joint

triceps muscle
this is the extensor muscle, which straightens the joint

scapula
(shoulder blade)

ball and socket joint

tendons
strong, non-stretch fibres, which attach the muscles to bones, enabling the muscles to move the joint

hinge joint

radius   ulna

Test yourself

1 What are the jobs of a) ligaments b) tendons?

2 Give an example of a flexor muscle and explain what it does.

3 Explain why muscles are often arranged in antagonistic pairs.

4 Why is it an advantage for an animal to be able to move?

Humans as organisms

Check the facts

A girl is born with all the **eggs** she will ever need in her **ovaries**.

After **puberty**, the eggs are released regularly from the ovaries and travel into the **oviducts**.

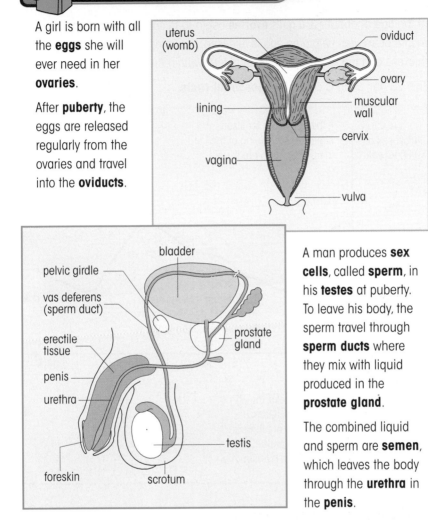

A man produces **sex cells**, called **sperm**, in his **testes** at puberty. To leave his body, the sperm travel through **sperm ducts** where they mix with liquid produced in the **prostate gland**.

The combined liquid and sperm are **semen**, which leaves the body through the **urethra** in the **penis**.

When a man and a woman have **sexual intercourse** the man's penis is stiffened by blood collecting inside it and he places his penis in the woman's **vagina**. The man then releases millions of sperm into the vagina.

The sperm swim though the **uterus** to the oviduct where one fuses with an egg. This is **fertilisation**.

Test yourself

1 Where are eggs stored before being released?

2 How many sperm are needed to fertilise an egg?

3 Where, in the female's reproductive system, does fertilisation take place?

BBC KS3 Check and Test: Science

Humans as organisms

Check the facts

At the age of about 13, a girl's **ovaries** begin to release an **egg** every month or so. Just before an egg is released, the lining of the **uterus** thickens and many tiny **blood vessels** form within the lining.

This 28-day cycle is called the **menstrual cycle**.

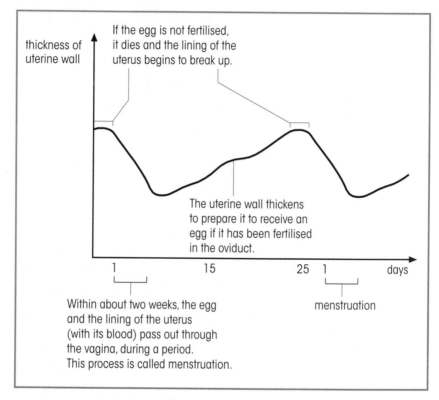

thickness of uterine wall

If the egg is not fertilised, it dies and the lining of the uterus begins to break up.

The uterine wall thickens to prepare it to receive an egg if it has been fertilised in the oviduct.

1   15   25   1   days

Within about two weeks, the egg and the lining of the uterus (with its blood) pass out through the vagina, during a period. This process is called menstruation.

menstruation

Test yourself

1 What happens to the lining of the uterus just before eggs are released from the ovaries?

2 About how long is a complete menstrual cycle in a woman?

3 What happens to an egg if it is not fertilised?

www.bbc.co.uk/revision

Check the facts

Once an egg has been **fertilised** it divides many times as it passes down the **fallopian tube** to the **uterus** and becomes an **embryo**, which sinks into the lining of the uterus.

After six weeks, the embryo is about 1.5 cm long. It has a brain and a heart. It lies in a liquid-filled bag, called the **amnion**, which protects it from jolts and bumps.

An **umbilical cord** links the embryo to a special organ, called the **placenta**, which has developed on the **uterus lining**.

The embryo's blood circulates through the placenta. As it does so, it absorbs **digested** food and **oxygen** from the mother's blood and releases **carbon dioxide** and other **waste materials** into it.

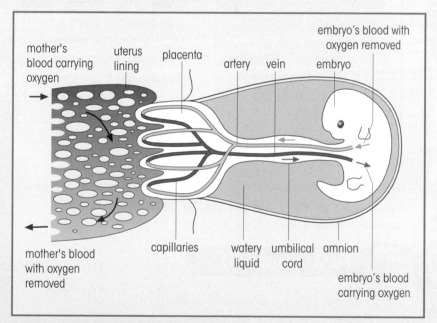

The mother's **blood system** and that of the embryo are separate, but are so close together that materials can pass between the two by **diffusion**.

Two months after **fertilisation**, the embryo is now called a **foetus** and continues its development for another seven months.

Test yourself

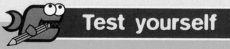

1 What is the job of the amnion?

2 What joins the embryo to the placenta?

Humans as organisms

BBC KS3 Check and Test: Science

Humans as organisms

Check the facts

Puberty is the time when a girl's body is able to produce a baby and when a boy's body is able to produce sperm.

Around age 13, girls begin their **menstrual cycles** and **menstruation** (periods) begin. Pubic hair begins to grow, as well as hair in the armpits. Breasts begin to develop and the hips widen. The **uterus** and **vagina** also begin to become larger.

In boys, puberty tends to start about a year later than in girls. Pubic hair begins to grow, as well as hair in the armpits. The **penis** and **testes** grow larger and mature **sperm** are produced. The shoulders broaden and the **voice box** becomes bigger, causing the voice to become deeper.

Puberty is part of **adolescence**.

Besides physical changes, emotional changes also take place. For example, both boys and girls have a greater sense of independence and an increased interest in the opposite sex.

Test yourself

1 What signs of puberty are the same in both boys and girls?

2 What is the average age for the beginning of puberty in:
 a) girls?
 b) boys?

3 During adolescence, boys' bodies change. Describe two of these changes.

Check the facts

Breathing takes place in the lungs when oxygen is added to the blood and carbon dioxide is removed.

The lungs are two spongy bags of tissue filled with millions of tiny **air sacs**, called **alveoli**.

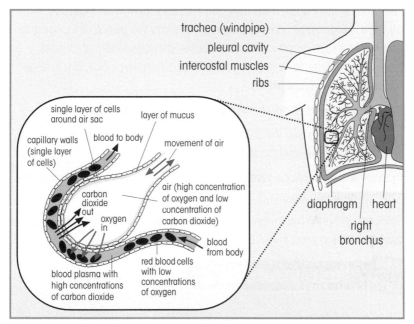

Alveoli have very thin walls and are surrounded by a dense network of **blood capillaries**, which are the smallest blood tubes in the body.

Oxygen, from the air you breathe, diffuses through the thin walls and into the blood. At the same time, carbon dioxide diffuses from the blood into the alveoli.

The alveoli lie at the ends of a mass of branching air passages, which connect with the **windpipe**, which is also know as the **trachea**.

Test yourself

1 In the lungs, which gas is:
   a) taken into the blood?   b) taken out of the blood.

2 State the features of the alveoli that make them good at their job.

3 What is the name given to the process by which gases pass in and out of blood capillaries?

Humans as organisms

Check the facts

Normally, tiny hair-like **cilia** line the breathing tubes. They trap dust and move in a wave-like fashion, backwards and forwards, carrying the dust towards the throat and mouth where it is swallowed. When the dust from smoking collects in the **lungs** it is coughed up – hence the term 'smoker's cough'.

Some of the dust stays in the lungs and irritates them. Eventually the **air sacs** are damaged and **bacteria** can get into the alveoli cells, causing **bronchitis**. If dust in tobacco smoke causes damage to lots of air sacs, many large spaces form and fill up with liquid from the lungs. This causes a disease called **emphysema**.

Tar in cigarettes contains chemicals that can cause **lung cancer**.

Tar deposits can cause the cilia to clump together, reducing their effectiveness at keeping the lungs clean.

Tobacco smoke contains **nicotine**. Nicotine interferes with the way in which lungs clean themselves of dust particles.

Smoking damages the inside of the breathing tubes and the **alveoli**, making breathing more difficult.

Test yourself

1 Name three lung diseases caused by smoking.

2 Describe the lungs' natural way of cleaning themselves. Why does this system fail in smokers?

3 Name a disease caused by tar in cigarettes.

4 How can smokers damage the health of non-smokers?

Check the facts

Respiration is not the same as **breathing**.

> **Breathing is the physical process of exchanging gases by diffusion. This requires special surfaces, such as alveoli in our lungs. Fish use gills as the surface to exchange gases.**

> **Respiration is the chemical release of energy from glucose sugar in every living cell of every living organism.**

Most energy is released when **oxygen** is used for respiration. This is called **oxidation** and is represented by the following word equation:

> **glucose + oxygen → carbon dioxide + oxygen + lots of energy**

Carbon dioxide and water vapour are the **waste products** of the chemical reaction between glucose and oxygen. After passing from the cells to the **lungs**, these waste products are breathed out.

Some living things can release a small amount of energy from glucose without using oxygen. This is called **anaerobic respiration**. Yeast is an example of a fungus made of one cell and it releases energy as follows:

> **glucose → carbon dioxide + ethanol (alcohol) + some energy**

Test yourself

1 What is the difference between the terms 'respiration' and 'breathing'?

2 Where does respiration take place?

3 State two ways in which aerobic respiration differs from anaerobic respiration.

4 Name a breathing surface that some animals use, besides lungs.

Humans as organisms

BBC KS3 Check and Test: Science

Check the facts

Oxygen from the air cannot travel further than the **air sacs** without entering the **blood system**. It does this by a process called **diffusion**.

> **Diffusion is the random net movement of particles from a region of high concentration to a region of low concentration until a state of equilibrium is achieved.**

There are more oxygen molecules in the air sacs than in the blood, so the oxygen molecules diffuse into the blood.

Red blood cells contain a red substance called **haemoglobin**. When there are lots of **oxygen** molecules present, haemoglobin collects them and becomes **oxyhaemoglobin**. This carries the oxygen to cells which need it for **respiration**.

Cells need oxygen when it is in short supply and, under these conditions, oxyhaemoglobin breaks down and releases oxygen.

Waste **carbon dioxide** is in high concentration in cells because they are respiring. It diffuses into the blood and is carried to the air sacs where it diffuses out.

Test yourself

1 What chemical carries oxygen in the red blood cells?

2 What is meant by diffusion?

3 Complete this word equation:

oxygen + haemoglobin → _____

4 What is the difference between:
   a) the amount of oxygen in air breathed in and air breathed out?
   b) the amount of carbon dioxide in air breathed in and air breathed out?

Check the facts

> **A drug is any chemical that alters the way in which you behave and which interferes with the normal chemical reactions that take place in the body.**

All dangerous drugs affect the way in which the brain and nerves work. Most are illegal to use unless they are prescribed by a doctor. Addiction to drugs, such as alcohol and tobacco, can often begin as a social habit but can then lead to serious dependence.

> **Addiction means that people are so dependent on a drug that their health and behaviour are affected if they do not have the drug.**

Alcohol and tobacco are common drugs that may lead to addiction.

Alcohol is a dangerous drug because it has a powerful effect on the **nervous system**. It slows down reaction times and gives a person a feeling of well-being, which may affect sensible judgement.

Long-term excessive drinking of alcohol causes damage to the heart, blood vessels, liver, kidneys and brain.

Test yourself

1 Why is it dangerous to drive a car after drinking alcohol?

2 What is meant by the word 'drug'.

3 What is meant by the term 'addiction'?

4 Which system of the body is affected by all drugs?

Humans as organisms

Check the facts

> **Immunity** is the ability of the body to resist disease naturally or artificially.

The best method of fighting a disease is by using the natural **immune system** in your blood.

Disease-causing **microbes** are called **pathogens** and include **viruses**, **bacteria**, some single-celled animals and **fungi**.

The body's natural immune system consists of special **white blood cells**. There are many types of these:

Some can make chemicals to fight the poisons produced by microbes.	Some can make proteins, called **antibodies**, which will react with **proteins**, called **antigens**, on the surface of microbes	Some can surround bacteria and digest them

Sometimes, people who catch a particular disease (e.g. chickenpox) will develop immunity against that disease and they won't become **infected** again. This is because their immune system remembers being attacked before and has antibodies to fight any further infection.

Test yourself

1 What types of cells are responsible for a natural immunity?

2 What do these cells produce to react with antigens found on microbes?

3 What is meant by the term 'pathogen'?

4 Some childhood diseases are caused by microbes. They infect children once, but are rarely able to cause the disease a second time in the same person. Give an example of such a disease.

Check the facts

Immunisation results in artificial active immunity and often involves giving the body a complete disease-causing organism in a weakened or dead form.

Modern forms of immunisation may only use parts of the disease-causing organism rather than the complete organism.

After immunisation, no illness results but the body's natural defence system automatically begins to make antibodies. If an immunised person later meets the same disease-causing organism, the defence system acts at once to destroy the invader.

One disease, smallpox, has been totally wiped out on a worldwide scale because of mass immunisation programmes throughout the world.

Dead microbes can be used to immunise against **measles** and **cholera**.

Weakened **microbes** can be used to immunise against diseases, such as **polio** and **tuberculosis** (TB).

Parts of microbes are used to immunise against **influenza**. The outer coat of the influenza virus (the **antigen**) is separated from the rest and is injected.

Test yourself

1 Name two diseases which can be avoided by immunising with
   a) a weakened microbe
   b) a dead microbe.

2 What disease has been totally eliminated from the world as a result of mass immunisation?

3 What does an antigen react with to produce immunity?

Check the facts

Green plants need food in order to grow. They take in simple materials from the soil and air, turning them into food, using the energy in sunlight.

> **Green plants make their food by photosynthesis.**
> **This is a process that uses the energy from sunlight and**
> **changes it into energy that the plant uses to live, and which**
> **we sometimes use as chemical energy in food.**

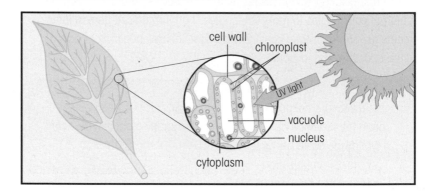

During photosynthesis, water drawn into the plant's roots from the soil is carried to the leaves. Here, **carbon dioxide** can get in from the air through tiny mouth-like holes, called **stomata**.

A green chemical, called **chlorophyll**, is found in the leaves and stems of plants and it is this chemical that absorbs the Sun's rays and helps to change light energy into stored chemical energy.

The energy from the Sun is used to make many chemical reactions take place in the leaf cells. These complex chemical reactions are summarised by the following word equation:

> **carbon dioxide + water + light energy → food + oxygen**

Test yourself

1 Name three chemicals needed for photosynthesis.

2 What is the main energy change in photosynthesis?

3 Which of the chemicals needed for photosynthesis are found in:
   a) the soil?   b) the air?

Green plants as organisms

Check the facts

Growth in plants not only results in an increase in size, but also in the development of special components, called **tissues** and **organs**, which are used for special purposes.

Cells

In order to grow, all living things have some **cells**, which can divide, increase in size, and then divide again. In this way, a single **fertilised egg cell** may become millions of cells.

Tissues

Tissues are collections of similar cells, which work as a team to do a particular job. For example, the outer layer of a leaf – the **epidermis**.

Organs

Organs are collections of tissues, which work as a team to do the same job. For example, the stem, root and leaves are all organs.

In plants, cells divide in special growing regions. These regions are buds on stems, the tip of the root, and a region which causes growth in width.

In order to grow, plants need to make carbohydrates and proteins.

Test yourself

1 Give two examples of plant organs.

2 What has to happen to a cell before it grows into a tissue?

3 Where, in a plant, would you find growing regions?

4 In order to grow, plants need proteins and carbohydrates. Name the process that produces these.

BBC KS3 Check and Test: Science

Green plants as organisms

Check the facts

Soil is formed when rock is broken up into tiny **mineral** particles by water and the weather.

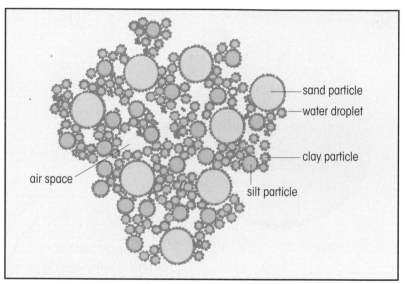

sand particle

water droplet

clay particle

air space

silt particle

Soil also contains air, water and **humus** (decaying plant and animal material). Soil provides a place for plants to live, acting as a source of water and minerals.

Water surrounding the soil particles has minerals dissolved in it. Both the water and the minerals can enter the plant as long as there is enough **oxygen** (in the air between the particles) for the roots to respire.

Too much water means there may not be enough air in the soil for the plant to **respire**, preventing plant growth.

Plants can make all the food classes except minerals, which they can only obtain from the soil.

The main minerals that plants need for growth are **nitrates, sulphates** and **phosphates**, which help to make protein. They also need **calcium**, **magnesium**, **sodium** and **potassium** for chemical reactions.

Test yourself

1 Why do plants need protein?

2 Name two minerals that plants need to make protein.

3 Why do roots die in soil that has been flooded for a long time?

4 What is meant by the term 'humus'?

www.bbc.co.uk/revision

Check the facts

A **species** is a group of living things that can breed to produce young. The young will grow up and be able to breed themselves.

Members of the same species do not all look the same – they vary. Their **variations** are sometimes due to the effects of their surroundings. These variations are due to the environment.

> **We all look similar but we are
> different because of two reasons:**
> • **the features we have inherited**
> • **the environment in which we live.**

For example, two identical pea seeds from the same pod had the same parents. Even if they have inherited the same features from both parents, they could still be different due to their environments. If one pea seed is grown in poor quality soil and with little water or light it will not grow as well as the other (grown in good soil with plenty of water and light), and will be small and weak.

Test yourself

1 Which two factors control how tall you will grow?

2 What must all members of a group of living things have to be able to do to be called a species?

3 What do you understand by the term 'environment'?

4 When a horse is crossed with a donkey, it produces a mule, which can never be a parent. When a labrador dog is crossed with a spaniel, it produces puppies, which can become parents. Explain why a horse and a donkey are two separate species but a Labrador and a spaniel are the same species.

Check the facts

Some variation between members of the same species is due to features being passed from parents to their young through inheritance.

The study of the ways these features are inherited is called **genetics**.

Inherited features are the result of the ways that **genes** behave in all living cells.

Some genes have a code, which tells the body to produce a particular colour of eyes; there are others for the colour of hair. Some gene codes tell the body how to produce chemicals, which control how we carry out all the characteristics of living things.

Genes are handed down from parents to their young when sperm cells **fertilise** egg cells.

In our bodies, genes are stored as identical pairs and all organisms have a fixed number of pairs of genes, depending on their species. One set comes from the father and the other comes from the mother. The types of genes we inherit control what we are.

Sometimes genes are faulty and this causes inherited diseases:

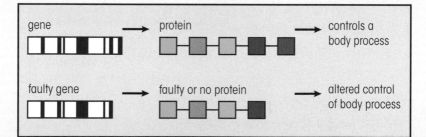

Test yourself

1 What is the name of the study of inheritance?

2 What are responsible for controlling features that can be inherited?

3 What causes inherited disease?

4 What is meant by the term 'fertilisation'?

Check the facts

Over thousands of years humans have made big changes to animals and plants by **selective breeding**.

Today's farm animals, and most of our pets, are the results of breeding individuals which show features that we find useful or attractive. Selective breeding all depends on the fact that animals born from the same parents will vary.

> For example, in a flock of lambs, some will have thicker wool than others. These could be selected to breed from, rather than to eat, and their young might all have thick wool. If this process is repeated, flocks of high-quality, wool-producing sheep are formed.

By using the same methods, humans have produced herds of dairy cows, fast race horses and over-weight turkeys. The vast range of dogs that exist show the possibilities of selective breeding.

Our **cultivated** cereal crops have all been developed in the same way from wild grasses, and many of the vegetables we eat have been developed from weedy looking plants normally growing on salt marshes near the sea.

Test yourself

1 What types of plants have been used to develop cereal crops?

2 Upon what does all selective breeding depend?

3 Name three features of farm animals that have been developed over thousands of years of selective breeding.

Variation and inheritance

Classification

Check the facts

Living things are divided into **kingdoms**.

Many living things can be placed in the plant kingdom or the animal kingdom. Some do not fit into either, so scientists place these in groups, such as **fungi**, **bacteria**, **viruses**, and organisms made of one cell.

The kingdoms are each divided into smaller groups called **divisions** (phyla). The organisms in any one division will have many features in common. For example, **vertebrates** all have backbones.

The divisions are then divided into **classes**. For example, the classes of the vertebrates are: fish, amphibia, reptiles, birds, and mammals.

The classes are divided into **orders**. For example, humans are mammals and are in the primate order, to which monkeys and apes also belong.

Orders are made up of groups of **families**. Lilies belong to the Liliaceae family.

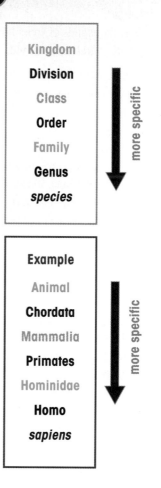

Kingdom
Division
Class
Order
Family
Genus
species

more specific

Example
Animal
Chordata
Mammalia
Primates
Hominidae
Homo
sapiens

more specific

All living things are given two names, usually based on ancient Latin or Greek. For example, humans are called Homo *sapiens*. Homo is Latin for 'man', and this is the **genus** name. *Sapiens* is Latin for 'wise', and this is the species name.

Test yourself

1 How many classes of vertebrates are there?

2 To which group of mammals do humans belong?

3 Name one feature that all vertebrates have.

4 Of all the types of animals mentioned on this page, which type do humans resemble the most?

Check the facts

The plant kingdom is made up of algae, mosses and liverworts, ferns, conifers and flowering plants.

All algae have **chlorophyll**. They must either live in water or in very moist conditions. Algae don't have proper leaves, stems, roots, or seeds. Algae also include seaweeds.

Mosses and liverworts live in very moist conditions but mosses can actually live on land. They have simple roots and leaves, but no seeds.

Ferns can live totally on land but are dependent on water for **fertilisation** as the male **sex cells** must swim to the female sex cells. They have large stems, roots, and leaf-like fronds. Some grow to the size of trees.

Conifers do not need water for fertilisation. They produce **cones** and have well-developed roots, stems, leaves and seeds but no flowers.

Flowering plants produce **pollen** from their flowers. Even grasses and plants without obvious flowers belong to this group. Besides having well-developed roots, stems and leaves, they produce seeds in fruits.

Test yourself

1 Which group of plants developed roots first?

2 What do all plants have in common to allow them to photosynthesise?

3 Which group of plants do you think is mostly responsible for the condition called 'hay fever', which is caused by pollen?

Classification

BBC KS3 Check and Test: Science

Classification

Check the facts

Vertebrates

All vertebrates have backbones and skeletons on the inside.
They include:

fish	cold-blooded, gills, paired fins, biting jaws
amphibians	cold-blooded, slimy skins, lay eggs in water
reptiles	cold-blooded, scaly skins, lay eggs on land
birds	warm-blooded, feathers
mammals	warm-blooded, hair, produce milk for their young.

Invertebrates

No invertebrates have backbones. Some of the main groups are:

protozoa	made of only one cell
jellyfish and sea anemones	live in water, two-layered bodies, tentacles
annelids	ringed worms (e.g. earthworms and leeches)
arthropods	jointed-leg types (e.g. insects, spiders and crabs), skeletons outside of the body, jointed bodies and legs
molluscs	shelled animals, soft and unjointed bodies, often with a shell on the outside or inside, (e.g. snails, slugs, octopus, mussels).

Test yourself

1 To which group of vertebrates do the following belong:
   a) humans
   b) frogs
   c) snakes?

2 An unknown animal has just been discovered. It has scales, a backbone, four jointed legs and lays eggs, which it buries in the ground. It is known to be cold-blooded. To what main group does it belong?

Check the facts

Living things survive because their shapes, behaviour, and the ways their bodies work are adapted to their environment.

Examples of adaptation explain why animals and plants look like they do.

Cacti can live in very dry conditions because they can store water in their bodies and reduce the amount of water that is evaporated from them. Their leaves have reduced over time, to form spines.

Birds and bats show adaptations for flight, by having light bones that can support a large wing surface area.

Fish, whales, seals and penguins are adapted for moving through water because they are streamlined and use their limbs as paddles.

An arctic fox has smaller ears than a desert fox so that less heat escapes from the surface area. It also has white fur whereas the desert fox has sandy coloured fur.

Test yourself

1 Suggest why birds have different shaped beaks.

2 Suggest why arctic foxes are white and desert foxes are sandy coloured.

3 What do the skeletons of the wings of birds and bats have in common?

4 How do the spines help cacti to survive in dry climates?

The living environment

The living environment

Check the facts

A struggle is seen when too many organisms compete for too little food. For example, when one plant slowly dies because its neighbour is taller and shades it from sunlight.

Competition can occur between the members of a single **species** when more offspring are produced than can possibly survive.

If a species can produce large numbers of young which vary slightly, there is a good chance that some will survive in their particular surroundings. Members of the same species also compete for breeding partners. Over millions of years some animals have developed elaborate structures or colours to attract a mate. The peacock's tail is probably the best example of this.

Competition also occurs between different species, particularly when they rely on the same source of food. It can occur between animals or between plants.

> **Competition results in survival of the fittest to breed. This does not always mean the survival of the strongest. It might, for example, mean the survival of the best camouflaged.**

Test yourself

1 Give two examples of adaptations used to attract a mate, besides a peacock's tail.

2 Name two things that plants compete for, apart from light.

3 When does competition occur within the same species?

4 What is meant by 'survival of the fittest' in terms of competition?

Check the facts

> **Food webs are diagrams, used to show how energy flows between organisms in a particular habitat.**

Most animals eat more than one type of food and a food web shows how animals depend upon each other.

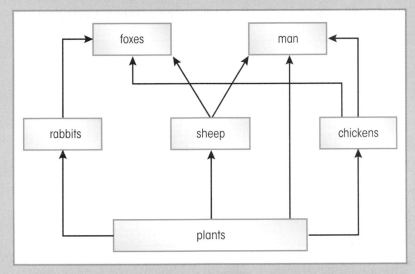

Anything that happens to one member in a food web will affect all the others. For instance, when a disease killed most of the rabbits in Britain, foxes were affected – they ate more farm animals. Also, more tree seedlings grew because fewer things were eating them.

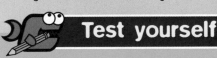

Test yourself

1 In food webs, what is represented by the arrows between species?

2 Why do food webs all begin with plants?

3 The above diagram could be a food web for a farm. Explain how the farmer would be affected if the rabbits were all killed by a disease.

Check the facts

Animals use only about one tenth of their food intake for bodybuilding. The energy from the rest is used for keeping warm or moving.

Much of the energy is wasted as heat, during respiration or in waste material in excretion.

The loss of energy at each stage of feeding can be shown in a pyramid:

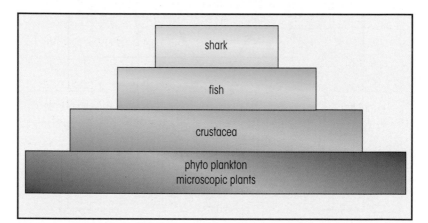

shark

fish

crustacea

phyto plankton
microscopic plants

It takes 1000 tonnes of microscopic plants to support one tonne of shark through the feeding stages.

Test yourself

1 What fraction of energy in food is used for growth?

2 State two ways in which energy is lost from a food pyramid.

3 How would you expect the numbers of individuals to alter, the further up the pyramid they appear?

Check the facts

There are vast numbers of tiny living organisms, called **microbes**, in our bodies, in the air, soil, water and plants.

> **Microbes can only be seen with a microscope. Some are essential to the lives of all other things and some can make useful things for us, while some can cause disease.**

Essential microbes include **bacteria** and **fungi**, which break down dead things and the waste from animals. By doing this they recycle **carbon**, **nitrogen**, **sulphur** and **phosphorus** so that they can be used by plants and animals.

The helpful microbes include yeast, which is used in bread-making and alcohol production. There are bacteria that help in the making of cheese, yoghurt, and vinegar. Some fungi can be used as substitutes for meat.

Disease-causing microbes include **viruses**, some bacteria, fungi and some animals made from one cell.

> **Influenza** and **chickenpox** are caused by viruses. **Cholera** and food poisoning are caused by bacteria. **Ringworm** is caused by a fungus, and **malaria** is caused by a single-celled animal.

Test yourself

1 What do you understand by the term 'germs'?

2 Name two diseases caused by bacteria.

3 Name two types of food that are made with the help of microbes.

4 Explain why life as we know it would not be possible without certain types of bacteria.

The living environment

BBC KS3 Check and Test: Science

Classifying materials

Check the facts

All materials exist as a solid, liquid or gas.
Solid, liquid and gas are the three states of matter.

If a solid is heated it will eventually **melt** into a liquid.

The temperature at which a solid turns into a liquid is the **melting point**.

Each solid has its own melting point. The melting point of ice is 0°C (**degrees Celsius**).

Similarly, each liquid has its own **boiling point** – the temperature at which it changes to a gas. The boiling point of water is 100°C.

Each solid, liquid or gas also has its own **density**.

Density is a measure of the amount of matter packed into a space.

It is measured in g/cm³. This is found by measuring the mass (in grams) of 1 cm³ of the material.

$$\text{density (g/cm}^3) = \frac{\text{mass (g)}}{\text{volume (cm}^3)}$$

Test yourself

1 Name the three states of matter.

2 What is melting?

3 What is boiling?

4 What is meant by 'the melting point of a solid'?

5 What is density?

6 A sample of solid X has a mass of 8 g and a volume of 6 cm³. Calculate the density of solid X. Show your working.

Check the facts

All matter, whether solid, liquid or gas, is made up of particles.

Solids

In a solid, the particles are packed tightly together in an organised structure.

Strong **forces** between the particles hold them in the structure.

The particles **vibrate** within their positions but don't move to different positions.

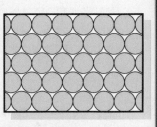

Liquids

The forces between particles in a liquid are weaker than those between particles in a solid.

This allows the particles to move randomly from place to place with space between them.

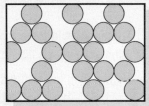

Gases

The **inter-particle forces** are very weak indeed.

The particles move randomly and quickly in all directions. There is a lot of space between them.

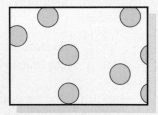

Test yourself

1 Do each of the following statements describe solids, liquids or gases?
  a) Particles have lots of space between them.
  b) Fairly weak forces between particles.
  c) Particles in a structure.
  d) Strong forces between particles.
  e) Particles vibrating in a fixed place.
  f) Particles moving very quickly in all directions.

2 Explain the meaning of:
  a) vibrating particles
  b) random movement
  c) inter-particle forces.

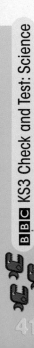

Classifying materials

Check the facts

Solids

> Because particles in a solid are fixed in place, solids do not flow, and have a fixed shape and volume.

Heating particles provides them with more energy. They **vibrate** increasingly until they break away and move about. This is **melting**. The solid has changed **state** and become a liquid.

Liquids

> Because particles in liquids move about, liquids flow and take the shape of their container.

Inter-particle forces are strong enough to prevent particles escaping and therefore liquids have a fixed volume.

By heating the particles, they gain enough energy to escape from the body of liquid. This is **boiling**. The liquid has changed state to gas.

Gases

> Because particles in gases move in all directions, gases have neither fixed volume nor fixed shape.

Particles hitting the sides of the container exert **gas pressure**.

Particles spread out and completely fill a container, taking on its shape. This process is called **diffusion**.

Test yourself

1 Explain why:
   a) solids do not flow
   b) gases completely fill their container
   c) liquids flow
   d) liquids have fixed volume.

2 What is diffusion?

3 Give four examples of changes of state.

4 Why does gas pressure increase as a gas is heated?

www.bbc.co.uk/revision

Check the facts

> A physical change is one in which no new substances are formed and which can easily be reversed by changing the conditions.

Changes of **state** are examples of physical change.

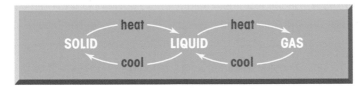

In each change of state, the **form** of the material changes but the **substance** is the same throughout.

Changes of **state** can be reversed.

Making **solutions** is also a physical change.

Salt in water produces a solution that tastes like salt and looks like water but no new substance is formed. The change is easily reversed by **evaporating** the water.

In physical changes, **mass** is conserved (unchanged).

Example

100 g of ice melts to form 100 g of water, and 100 g of water and 10 g of salt will form 110 g of solution.

Test yourself

1 What is a physical change?

2 Give two examples of physical change.

3 What weight of salt is needed to produce 135 g of salt solution from 100 g of water?

4 Which of these are physical changes. Explain your answers:
   a) stirring sugar in water
   b) frying an egg
   c) burning wood
   d) melting iron
   e) painting a wall
   f) folding paper?

Changing materials

BBC KS3 Check and Test: Science

Changing materials

Check the facts

Heating a liquid causes the temperature to rise until the **boiling point** is reached.

> **If heating continues once a liquid has reached boiling point, the temperature no longer rises.**

The **particles** use the extra heat energy above boiling point to overcome the **forces** holding them within the liquid. The heat is not being used to raise the temperature, which therefore remains constant.

When the gas is cooled to form a liquid, heat energy is released as **condensation**. Heating curves demonstrate this, as shown below:

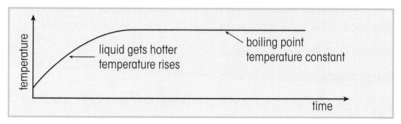

Heating solids has a similar effect.

Temperature is constant at **melting point**.

Further heating is used by particles to overcome forces holding them in the solid structure:

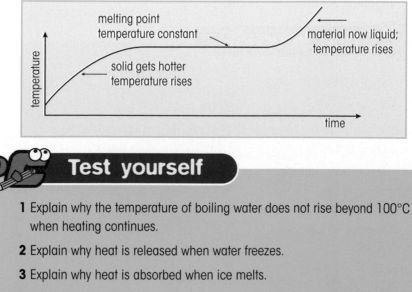

Test yourself

1 Explain why the temperature of boiling water does not rise beyond 100°C when heating continues.

2 Explain why heat is released when water freezes.

3 Explain why heat is absorbed when ice melts.

4 Explain why putting nail varnish remover on skin causes it to feel cold.

5 Draw a heating curve for heating ice from −20°C to +20°C.

Check the facts

Salt stirred in water dissolves to form a clear **solution**. Salt is the **solute** – the material that **dissolves**. Water is the **solvent** – the liquid in which the solute dissolves.

Solutions containing small amounts of solute are **dilute** solutions.

By adding more solute, the solution becomes more concentrated.

Eventually the solution becomes 'full' of solute and no more dissolves. This is a **saturated** solution.

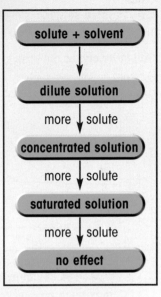

solute + solvent

↓

dilute solution

more ↓ solute

concentrated solution

more ↓ solute

saturated solution

more ↓ solute

no effect

Changing materials

Materials which dissolve in water are soluble (e.g. salt, sugar).

Materials which do not dissolve in water are insoluble (e.g. chalk, sand).

Test yourself

1 Explain the meaning of:
- a) solute
- b) solvent
- c) dilute solution
- d) concentrated solution
- e) saturated solution
- f) soluble
- g) insoluble.

2 How would you make a dilute solution into a concentrated solution?

3 Which of the following are solutions?
- a) fruit juice
- b) toothpaste
- c) tap water
- d) air
- e) sea water.

BBC KS3 Check and Test: Science

Changing materials

Check the facts

If a **saturated solution** is heated, the undissolved **solute** will **dissolve**. This is because, for most solutes, **solubility** increases with temperature.

Solubility curves are used to compare the solubility of substances under different conditions, such as temperature ranges, as shown below.

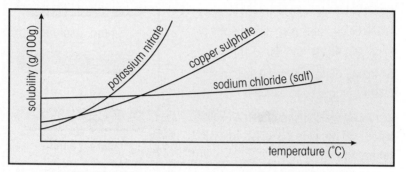

> **The solubility of a solute in a solvent is the maximum amount (g) of the solute that will dissolve in 100 g of the solvent at a particular temperature.**

Solubility curves show that different materials have different solubilities. For example, the solubility of salt in water at 25°C is 30 g / 100 g of water and the solubility of sugar at 25°C is 230 g / 100 g of water.

The most common solvent is water. It is cheap, safe, plentiful and dissolves many materials. Some materials are **insoluble** in water.

Some substances are soluble in other solvents, for example, ethanol dissolves ink, white spirit dissolves paint and paraffin dissolves tar.

Test yourself

1 Name four solvents.

2 Can water remove grease from clothes? Explain your answer.

3 Give the definition of solubility.

4 Using the solubilities of potassium nitrate, below, plot the solubility curve.

Temperature (°C)	0	20	40	60	80
Solubility (g/100 g)	12	33	65	104	155

5 What happens when a saturated solution of potassium nitrate is cooled from 40°C to 20°C? Use the information in question 4.

Check the facts

> **An element is a single material that cannot be broken down into simpler materials.**

Water can be split up into hydrogen and oxygen but the hydrogen and oxygen cannot be broken down any further. They are each single **substances**. They are elements.

All materials are made by combining the 90 naturally-occurring elements.

Each element has a symbol. Some of the common ones are listed below:

Aluminium	**Al**	Iron	**Fe**
Calcium	**Ca**	Nitrogen	**N**
Carbon	**C**	Oxygen	**O**
Chlorine	**Cl**	Potassium	**K**
Copper	**Cu**	Sodium	**Na**
Hydrogen	**H**	Zinc	**Zn**

All elements are made up of tiny **particles**, called **atoms**.

> **An atom is the smallest part of an element that can exist and all atoms of an element are alike. Different elements have different atoms.**

Test yourself

1 What is an element?

2 What is an atom?

3 What is the symbol for:
   a) sodium   b) hydrogen   c) calcium   d) iron?

4 State the name of:
   a) Zn   b) O   c) Cu   d) K.

5 Which elements make up water?

6 Find out which elements each of the following are made up of:
   a) common salt   d) sulphuric acid
   b) chalk   e) caustic soda
   c) lime-water   f) nitric acid.

Elements, compunds and mixtures

Check the facts

All **atoms** consist of three **sub-atomic particles protons neutrons** and **electrons**

> **All atoms of an element have the same number of protons and electrons. The number of neutrons can vary.**

The number of protons in an atom of an element is known as the **atomic number** of the element. It is used to identify the element.

The **periodic table** places elements in order of atomic number.

The table has vertical columns called groups. Elements in a group have similar properties to each other.

The periodic table for the first 20 elements is shown below.

			Hydrogen ← name				0
group number			H ← symbol				Helium
			1 ← number of protons				He
I	II	III	IV	V	VI	VII	2
Lithium	Beryllium	Boron	Carbon	Nitrogen	Oxygen	Fluorine	Neon
Li	Be	B	C	N	O	Fl	Ne
3	4	5	6	7	8	9	10
Sodium	Magnesium	Aluminium	Silicon	Phosphorus	Sulphur	Chlorine	Argon
Na	Mg	Al	Si	P	S	Cl	Ar
11	12	13	14	15	16	17	18
Potassium	Calcium						
K	Ca						
19	20						

Test yourself

1 Name the three sub-atomic particles.

2 What is meant by the 'atomic number of an element'?

3 From the periodic table, give the name and symbol of two elements in:
a) group I   b) group IV   c) group VII.

4 Give the name and symbol of an element with similar properties to:
a) sodium   b) magnesium   c) chlorine   d) neon.

5 How many protons are found in atoms of:
a) aluminium   b) fluorine   c) calcium   d) carbon.

Check the facts

Topic 42 showed that water can be split into two **elements**: hydrogen and oxygen. This is because water is first formed by combining hydrogen and oxygen. Water is a **compound**.

> **A compound is a pure material made up of two or more elements combined together.**

The table below lists some compounds and **minerals**, and the elements from which they are formed.

Compound:	Elements in compound:
water	hydrogen, oxygen
carbon dioxide	carbon, oxygen
magnesium oxide	magnesium, oxygen
sodium chloride (common salt)	sodium, chlorine
calcium carbonate (chalk)	calcium, carbon, oxygen
haematite (iron ore).	iron, oxygen.

Molecules

When elements combine to form compounds, the atoms of one element combine with the atoms of the other element(s) to form **molecules** of the compound.

> **A molecule is the smallest part of a compound and is made up of two or more atoms combined.**

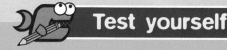

Test yourself

1 What is a compound?

2 Name four compounds not mentioned in question 4. State which elements each contains.

3 What is a molecule?

4 Name the elements in:
a) zinc oxide
b) calcium chloride
c) lead sulphide
d) potassium iodide
e) calcium bromide
f) magnesium carbonate.

Elements, compunds and mixtures

BBC KS3 Check and Test: Science

Elements, compunds and mixtures

Check the facts

Compounds are represented by a **formula**, made up from the symbols of the **elements** in the compound. Some examples are shown below.

Compound	Formula	Compound	Formula
water	H_2O	ammonia	NH_3
magnesium oxide	MgO	sulphuric acid	H_2SO_4
carbon dioxide	CO_2	sodium chloride (salt)	NaCl

The numbers show how many of each **atom** there are in a **molecule** of the compound. No number means there is one of that atom present.

Compound	Formula	Numbers of each type of atom
water	H_2O	2 hydrogen, 1 oxygen
ammonia	NH_3	1 nitrogen, 3 hydrogen
sulphuric acid	H_2SO_4	2 hydrogen, 1 sulphur, 4 oxygen

**A molecule of water always contains two hydrogen atoms and one oxygen atom.
The composition of each compound is fixed
– this is the law of constant composition.**

Test yourself

1 State the formula of:

a) water   b) sulphuric acid   c) sodium chloride   d) ammonia.

2 State how many of each atom are present in one molecule of:

a) carbon dioxide   b) magnesium oxide   c) common salt.

3 Copy and complete the table:

Formula	Name	Numbers of each type of atom
Al_2O_3		
$CaCl_2$		
$ZnSO_4$		

4 Explain the law of constant composition.

Elements, compunds and mixtures

Check the facts

Most substances are not pure materials. They are **mixtures** of materials.

> **In a mixture, the materials are jumbled together but are not chemically combined.**

A mixture does not have a fixed composition. Any amount of each material can be used to make a mixture.

A mixture is not a new material with new properties. It has the properties of its constituents and is easily separated back into those constituents

For more on separating mixtures, see topic 47.

Some examples of mixtures are: air, sea water, rocks, soil, most foods, blood, cosmetics and medicines.

It is important to know the difference between mixtures and **compounds**:

Mixtures:	Compounds:
constituents not combined	elements combined together
no new material formed – mixtures have the properties of their constituents	compounds are new materials with properties of their own, not the properties of their elements
easily separated	very difficult to separate into their elements
no fixed composition	fixed composition

Test yourself

1 What is a mixture?

2 Divide the following into mixtures and pure elements or compounds:

a) salt water
b) pizza
c) oxygen
d) air
e) petrol
f) toothpaste
g) steam
h) aluminium
i) tap water
j) lipstick.

3 List the differences between a mixture and a compound.

BBC KS3 Check and Test: Science

Elements, compunds and mixtures

Check the facts

Because the constituents of a mixture are not
combined together, they are easily separated.

Four methods of separation are shown in the diagrams below.

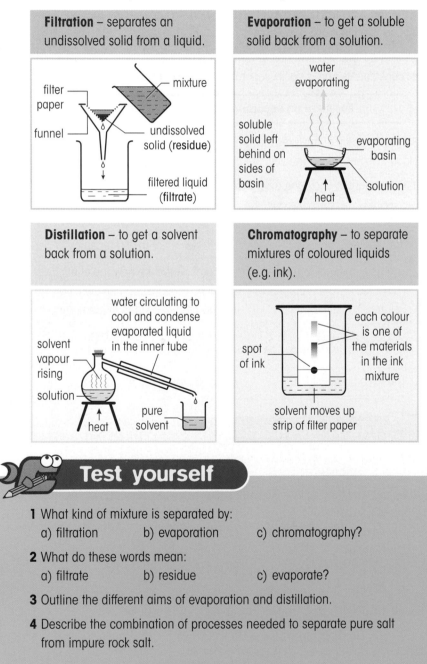

Filtration – separates an
undissolved solid from a liquid.

filter paper
funnel
mixture
undissolved solid (**residue**)
filtered liquid (**filtrate**)

Evaporation – to get a soluble
solid back from a solution.

water evaporating
soluble solid left behind on sides of basin
evaporating basin
solution
heat

Distillation – to get a solvent
back from a solution.

water circulating to cool and condense evaporated liquid in the inner tube
solvent vapour rising
solution
heat
pure solvent

Chromatography – to separate
mixtures of coloured liquids
(e.g. ink).

spot of ink
each colour is one of the materials in the ink mixture
solvent moves up strip of filter paper

Test yourself

1 What kind of mixture is separated by:
a) filtration   b) evaporation   c) chromatography?

2 What do these words mean:
a) filtrate   b) residue   c) evaporate?

3 Outline the different aims of evaporation and distillation.

4 Describe the combination of processes needed to separate pure salt
from impure rock salt.

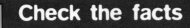
Check the facts

> Changes that cannot be reversed and produce
> entirely new materials are chemical changes.
> Chemical changes are brought about
> by chemical reactions.

Chemical reactions are vital to everyday life. The majority of materials we use – fabrics, foods, medicines, plastics, fuels, fertilisers – are made by chemical reactions.

In a chemical reaction, the starting materials are the **reactants** and the materials at the finish are the **products**.

Reactions proceed by using the **atoms** of the reactant molecules and re-assembling them to make the product **molecules**.

Because the same atoms are used and atoms are not made or lost:

> total mass of products = total mass of reactants

> This leads to the law of conservation of mass,
> which states that matter is neither created nor
> destroyed in a chemical reaction.

Test yourself

1 Explain:
   a) reactant
   b) product
   c) conservation of mass.

2 State two characteristics of chemical change.

3 Explain why burning paper and baking a cake are both chemical changes.

4 Explain why mass is constant throughout a chemical reaction.

5 1.2 g of magnesium burn in oxygen to produce 2.0 g of magnesium oxide. What weight of oxygen is used?

Chemical change

BBC KS3 Check and Test: Science

Chemical change

Check the facts

> All chemical reactions can be
> represented by a word equation.
> The word equation gives the names of
> all reactants and products.

For example, when magnesium burns in oxygen, magnesium oxide is produced. The word equation for this is:

magnesium + oxygen → magnesium oxide

When hydrochloric acid is poured onto pieces of zinc, zinc chloride and hydrogen are produced. The word equation for this is:

zinc + hydrochloric acid → zinc chloride + hydrogen

Test yourself

1 Write word equations for each of the following reactions:
   a) making water from hydrogen and oxygen
   b) burning sodium in oxygen to make sodium oxide
   c) adding calcium oxide to water to make calcium hydroxide
   d) making magnesium sulphate and hydrogen by adding sulphuric acid to magnesium.

2 When hydrochloric acid is added to calcium carbonate, bubbles of carbon dioxide are given off and calcium chloride and water are left.
   a) Name the reactants.
   b) Name the products.
   c) Write a word equation for the reaction.

3 Copy and complete the following word equations:

   a) sodium + chlorine → _____ _____

   b) zinc + _____ acid → zinc chloride + _____

   c) magnesium sulphate + potassium hydroxide →
      magnesium hydroxide + _____ _____

   d) potassium + _____ → potassium oxide.

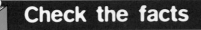
Check the facts

**All living things are maintained by chemical reactions,
such as: digestion, respiration and photosynthesis.**

Digestion

Before eaten food can react with breathed in **oxygen**, to produce energy
by **respiration**, it must be digested.

Once the food is broken down by chewing and by the action of stomach
acids, it undergoes chemical reactions with **enzymes**. This breaks it down
further into molecules that are small enough to enter the bloodstream.

large food molecules + enzymes → small food molecules

This chemical reaction is digestion.

Respiration

Digested food and breathed-in oxygen react in the bloodstream:

food + oxygen → carbon dioxide + water + energy
breathed out   *used by body*

Photosynthesis

Photosynthesis is the process by which plants make their food.

Carbon dioxide from air, and water from soil, are absorbed by **chlorophyll**
in leaves. Energy from the Sun converts this to **glucose** sugar.

$$\textbf{carbon dioxide + water} \xrightarrow[\text{sunlight}]{\text{chlorophyll}} \textbf{glucose + oxygen}$$

Glucose provides food for plants and also for the animals that eat plants.

Oxygen is released into the atmosphere.

Test yourself

1 What part do enzymes play in digestion. Why is this process necessary?

2 Explain the chemical reaction plants undergo to make food.

3 What is respiration?

4 Are respiration and breathing the same process? Explain your answer.

Chemical change

BBC KS3 Check and Test: Science

Chemical change

Check the facts

> **Most of the articles we use are made from materials that are created during chemical reactions. These materials are usually one of: plastic, glass, fibres, ceramic, metal. Each of these is made by chemical reaction.**

Some chemical reactions occur naturally.

Some of these reactions are welcome and produce helpful results, such as fruit ripening, glue setting, food cooking and so on.

Other natural reactions are not so welcome and produce unhelpful results, such as iron rusting and food rotting.

Unwelcome reactions can be prevented.

Iron goes rusty in contact with both air and water. Keeping iron away from air and water helps to prevent rusting.

Food rots in warm, moist air and in contact with bacteria. Keeping food cold, out of moist air and away from bacteria keeps it fresher longer.

 ## Test yourself

1 Name the five types of material from which most things are made.

2 Give one example of an article of each type in use in your home.

3 Explain how painting prevents iron rusting.

4 Name three methods of keeping food fresh.

5 Why do unpeeled apples not go brown?

6 Why do iron goal posts rust from the bottom up?

Chemical change

Check the facts

Fossil fuels were formed millions of years ago from **decaying** animal and plant remains.

Coal, gas and oil are fossil fuels.

> **Fuels are burned to obtain heat.**
> **The other main products are carbon dioxide and water:**
> **fossil fuel + oxygen → carbon dioxide + water + heat**

Some fossil fuels also produce sulphur dioxide and nitrogen dioxide.

All these gases pass into the atmosphere where they dissolve in rainfall to form acids:

> **carbon, sulphur or nitrogen dioxides + water → acid rain**

Acid rain damages plant and pond life and causes chemical weathering to buildings and metal structures.

Acid rain can be prevented by stopping acid gases getting into the air.

This means either absorbing them in some way after the fuel has been burnt, or finding alternative fuels.

Test yourself

1 Explain the meaning of the following:
   a) fuel
   b) fossil fuels
   c) air pollution.

2 Name two fossil fuels.

3 How is acid rain formed? State two harmful effects of acid rain.

4 How can electric vehicles reduce air pollution?

5 Why do areas away from industrial cities suffer the effects of acid rain?

6 Find out what 'renewable energy' means. Name three sources of renewable energy.

BBC KS3 Check and Test: Science

The greenhouse effect

Chemical change

 **Check the facts**

The amount of carbon dioxide in the atmosphere is slowly increasing.

One of the main reasons for this is the vast amounts of **fossil fuels** that are being burned.

Another reason is that the trees and plants in rain forests, which absorb carbon dioxide from the atmosphere, are being cut down at a high rate.

> **Carbon dioxide is a heavy gas which remains in the atmosphere and traps heat in. As carbon dioxide levels increase, the temperature of the earth slowly increases as well. This is called the greenhouse effect and carbon dioxide is a greenhouse gas.**

Fossil fuels also produce sulphur dioxide and nitrogen dioxide. These are both greenhouse gases.

Another greenhouse gas which is increasing is methane. This is produced by rotting waste and vegetable matter, and from sewage.

Test yourself

1 Name four greenhouse gases.

2 Explain the greenhouse effect.

3 Outline two reasons for the present increase in the greenhouse effect.

4 Why might the amount of methane in the atmosphere be increasing?

5 Suggest three ways in which mankind might be able to decrease the greenhouse effect.

Check the facts

There are 90 naturally-occurring elements – 69 of these are metals.

Metals are usually:

- solids at room temperature with high **melting points** and **densities**
- good **conductors** of heat and electricity
- **malleable** (can be beaten into shapes)
- **ductile** (can be stretched into wires)
- shiny, if polished.

Common exceptions:

- mercury is a liquid at room temperature
- sodium and potassium are soft and have low melting points and low densities
- aluminium is light but strong and has a low density.
- Iron is the only common metal that is magnetic. Most metals are not magnetic.

Metals and non-metals

Test yourself

1 Explain:
   a) malleable
   b) ductile
   c) conductor of electricity
   d) conductor of heat.

2 Name the metal that is liquid at room temperature.

3 State whether each of the following is magnetic or not:
   a) copper   b) lead   c) iron.

4 For each of the following metals, state two properties it must have to be used as stated:
   a) iron for horseshoes
   b) copper for electrical wires
   c) aluminium for saucepans
   d) aluminium for mirrors.

BBC KS3 Check and Test: Science

Metals and non-metals

Check the facts

The 21 non-metals have physical properties that are common to them all. The list below shows the properties of non-metals. Look back at topic 54 and see how they are different from those of metals.

Non-metals are:

- light elements with low **melting** and **boiling points**
- low in **density**
- varied in their **physical state** at room temperature – 11 are gases (e.g. hydrogen, oxygen, nitrogen), 9 are solids (e.g. sulphur, carbon), 1 is a liquid (bromine)
- poor **conductors** of heat and electricity
- neither **malleable** nor **ductile** (solid non-metals are brittle and break when beaten)
- never **magnetic**.

Common exceptions:

- graphite (a form of carbon) is a good conductor of electricity
- diamond (another form of carbon) is the hardest natural substance known.

Test yourself

1 Name:
   a) a non-liquid that conducts electricity
   b) a liquid non-metal
   c) a solid non-metal
   d) a hard non-metal.

2 List three properties of non-metals and for each one state how metals behave in contrast.

3 State whether each of the following is a metal or a non-metal:
   a) element W – shiny solid, conducts electricity, melts at 950°C
   b) element X – used to make saucepans and electrical wiring
   c) element Y – gas, non-conductor of electricity
   d) element Z – solid, high melting point, does not conduct electricity.

www.bbc.co.uk/revision

Check the facts

> When metals burn in air or pure oxygen,
> the oxide of the metal is formed.
> In general, metal **+** oxygen **→** metal oxide.

Example

sodium + oxygen → sodium oxide

magnesium + oxygen → magnesium oxide

> When metals react with water, the hydroxide of the
> metal is formed and hydrogen is given off.
> In general, metal **+** water **→** metal hydroxide **+** hydrogen.

Example

sodium + water → sodium hydroxide+ hydrogen

calcium + water → calcium hydroxide + hydrogen

> Some metals will not react with water but will
> react with steam. In this case, the oxide of the
> metal is formed along with hydrogen.
> In general, metal **+** steam **→** metal oxide **+** hydrogen.

Example

zinc + steam → zinc oxide + hydrogen

iron + steam → iron oxide + hydrogen

> It should be noted that the oxides and
> hydroxides of metals are bases

For more information on bases, see topics 61 and 62.

Test yourself

1 Write word equations for the following reactions:

   a) sodium burning in oxygen

   b) magnesium burning in air

   c) potassium burning in oxygen

   d) sodium in water

   e) zinc in steam

   f) magnesium in steam

   g) potassium in water.

2 Write general word equations for:

   a) metals in oxygen   b) metals in water   c) metals in steam.

Metals and non-metals

Check the facts

Magnesium reacts easily with dilute hydrochloric acid to produce magnesium chloride solution and hydrogen.

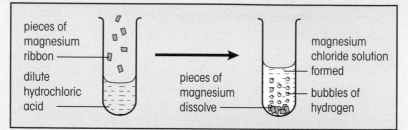

pieces of magnesium ribbon

dilute hydrochloric acid

pieces of magnesium dissolve

magnesium chloride solution formed

bubbles of hydrogen

The word equation is:

magnesium + hydrochloric acid → magnesium chloride + hydrogen

Magnesium chloride is a **salt**. It is formed because the magnesium **displaces** (pushes out) the hydrogen in the acid and takes its place.

> **See topic 61 for more information on salt formation.**

A salt is a compound formed when the hydrogen of an acid is replaced by a metal. All metals above copper in the **reactivity series** will react like this with dilute acids.

> **See topic 58 for more information on the reactivity series.**

In general, metal + acid → salt + hydrogen

Example

zinc + sulphuric acid → zinc sulphate + hydrogen

Test yourself

1 What is meant by the terms 'salt' and 'displace'?
Give an example for each.

2 Write word equations for each of the following reactions:
 a) magnesium and dilute hydrochloric acid
 b) magnesium and dilute sulphuric acid
 c) zinc and dilute hydrochloric acid
 d) zinc and dilute sulphuric acid.

3 Name the salt formed from each of the following pairs:
 a) aluminium and sulphuric acid   c) iron and hydrochloric acid
 b) calcium and hydrochloric acid   d) magnesium and nitric acid.

Metals and non-metals

Check the facts

Metals may react with air, water and acids with different degrees of severity.

For more on these reactions see topics 56 and 57.

We can place metals in order of reactivity, to make the **reactivity series**.

	Metal	air/oxygen	water/steam	dilute acids
Most reactive	Potassium K	Burn in air – more vigorously in pure oxygen.	React in cold water to give hydroxide + hydrogen	Explosive and dangerous reaction
	Sodium Na			
	Calcium Ca			React to displace hydrogen and form the salt
	Magnesium Mg			
	Aluminium Al		React with steam to give oxide + hydrogen	
	Zinc Zn			
	Iron Fe			
	Lead Pb	Do not burn. Surface converted to oxide on heating in air	No reaction at all	Reacts slowly with warm acid
	Copper Cu			No reaction at all
	Silver Ag	No reaction at all		
Least reactive	Gold Au			

BBC KS3 Check and Test: Science

Test yourself

1 What is the reactivity series?

2 Answer the following using the reactivity series above.

a) Which are the most and least reactive metals?

b) Name two metals which do not corrode in air.

c) Name two metals that react with steam but not cold water.

d) Name three metals that react safely with dilute acids.

e) Name two metals that react with cold, dilute acid but not cold water.

Metals and non-metals

Check the facts

Pieces of zinc placed in blue copper sulphate solution gradually become coated with red-brown copper. The blue of the solution fades to colourless. The reaction that has taken place is:

zinc + copper sulphate → zinc sulphate + copper
| blue | colourless | red-brown |
| solution | solution | powder |

The zinc has **displaced** the copper because zinc is more reactive (higher in the **reactivity series**) than copper.

A more reactive metal displaces a less reactive metal from its solutions.

Example
magnesium + zinc sulphate → magnesium sulphate + zinc
iron + zinc sulphate → no reaction

A more reactive metal also displaces a less reactive metal from its oxide.

Example
aluminium + iron oxide → aluminium oxide + iron
copper + iron oxide → no reaction

Test yourself

1 Copy and complete these word equations:

a) magnesium + zinc oxide → _Magnesium oxide_ + _zinc_

b) zinc + _Copper_ _oxide_ → _Zinc_ oxide + copper

c)  _iron_ + _Magnesium oxide_ → magnesium oxide + iron

d) magnesium + copper chloride → _____ _____ + _____

e) iron + _____ nitrate → _____ _____ + lead.

2 For each pair below, write a word equation if you predict they will react and 'no reaction' if not:

a) lead + copper sulphate
b) magnesium + lead nitrate
c) zinc + aluminium chloride
d) zinc + lead oxide
e) magnesium + aluminium sulphate

f) copper + iron nitrate
g) silver + copper chloride
h) magnesium + aluminium oxide
i) copper + silver nitrate
j) gold + zinc chloride.

www.bbc.co.uk/revision

Check the facts

We can show whether a solution is an acid or not by adding an **indicator**, such as **litmus**.

Litmus turns red in acid.

All acids are not the same. Some are strong acids, e.g. hydrochloric, sulphuric, nitric acids. Others are weak acids, e.g. carbonic acid (fizzy drinks, acid rain), ethanoic acid (vinegar).

The strength of an acid is measured on the **pH scale**.

All acids have a pH lower than 7. The lower the pH, the stronger the acid.

pH 7 is neutral. Water is pH 7.

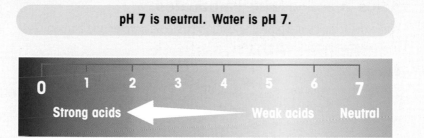

The indicator used to measure pH is **universal indicator**. This shows different colours in solutions of different pH.

The colour range is red (pH 0) → orange → yellow → green (pH 6)

Test yourself

1 Name two strong acids.

2 Name two weak acids.

3 What is an indicator?

4 What colour is litmus in acids?

5 What is the approximate pH range of:
   a) strong acids
   b) weak acids.

6 Lemon juice is acidic. What do you think its pH might be? Explain your answer.

Acids and bases

BBC KS3 Check and Test: Science

Acids and bases

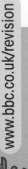

Check the facts

Students need to be familiar with three general reactions of acids.

Acids reacting with metals

When dilute acids are added to metals, a salt and hydrogen are formed.

Example

sulphuric acid + magnesium → magnesium sulphate + hydrogen.

acid + metal → salt + hydrogen

Acids reacting with carbonates

When dilute acids are added to carbonates, a salt, water and carbon dioxide are formed.

Example

nitric acid + sodium carbonate → sodium nitrate + water + carbon dioxide

acid + carbonate → salt + water + carbon dioxide

Acids reacting with bases

Bases are oxides and hydroxides of metals.
When dilute acids are added to bases, a salt and water are formed.

Example

copper oxide + sulphuric acid → copper sulphate + water

magnesium hydroxide + hydrochloric acid → magnesium chloride + water

acid + base → salt + water

Test yourself

1 The salts of sulphuric acid are sulphates. What are the salts of:
   a) hydrochloric acid?   b) nitric acid?

2 Write acid and base word equations to make:
   a) copper chloride   b) zinc sulphate

3 Write acid + carbonate word equations to make:
   a) potassium nitrate   b) magnesium sulphate

4 Write acid + metal word equations to make:
   a) iron sulphate   b) magnesium chloride

Check the facts

Bases are **oxides** and **hydroxides** of metals.

Bases react with acids to give salt and water.

> For more on base reactions see topic 61.

Bases are all solids and most of them are insoluble in water.

The few that do dissolve are **alkalis**.

> **An alkali is a soluble base.**

Two common alkalis are sodium hydroxide and potassium hydroxide.

Alkalis turn **litmus** blue and have a pH greater than 7. The higher the pH, the stronger the alkali.

The full pH scale goes from 0 to 14 as shown below.

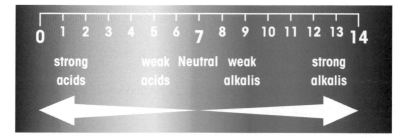

Universal indicator in alkalis is:

> **dark green (pH 8) → pale blue → blue → purple (pH 14)**

Test yourself

1 What is a base? Name two examples.

2 What is an alkali? Name two examples.

3 What effect do alkalis have on litmus?

4 What is the approximate pH range of: a) strong alkalis? b) weak alkalis?

5 What is a neutral solution?

6 Egg white is alkaline. What might its approximate pH be?
Explain your answer.

7 The pH of oven cleaner is 13. This information is on the packaging.
What else might it say on the packaging that relates to this information?

Check the facts

Like all **bases**, **alkalis** react with **acids** to make salt and water.

Example

hydrochloric acid + sodium hydroxide → sodium chloride + water

The solution formed is **neutral** (pH 7).

> **The reaction between an acid and an alkali is called neutralisation.**

Neutralisation has applications in everyday life, such as in gardening, in treating indigestion and in making fertilisers.

Soil

Most plants prefer soil of pH 6.5–7.5.
Adding peat (acidic) to alkaline soil, or lime (alkaline) to acidic soil corrects the pH by **neutralisation**.

Indigestion

Acidic foods (sauces, fizzy drinks) can increase the level of stomach acid and cause indigestion.
Indigestion remedies contain alkalis, such as bicarbonate of soda, which neutralise this excess acid.

Fertilisers

Nitrogenous fertilisers (ammonium nitrate, ammonium sulphate) are salts made by neutralisation.

ammonia (alkaline) + sulphuric acid → ammonium sulphate.
ammonia + nitric acid → ammonium nitrate.

Test yourself

1 What is neutralisation? Why is it given this title?

2 Write word equations for the following neutralisation reactions:
   a) sulphuric acid and sodium hydroxide
   b) nitric acid and potassium hydroxide.

3 Which material is used to neutralise
   a) acid soil?   b) alkaline soil?

4 Why do indigestion remedies contain bicarbonate of soda?

5 Write two word equations to convert ammonia into nitrogenous fertilisers.

Check the facts

Studying chemical reactions shows patterns that enable predictions to be made about other reactions.

Elements and compounds

When two **elements** combine a **compound** is formed.

Q   What happens when sodium reacts with chlorine?

A   Sodium and chlorine are both elements and therefore:

sodium + chlorine → sodium chloride

Q   What happens when calcium is burned in air?

A   **Combustion** combines the metal and oxygen into an oxide:

calcium + oxygen → calcium oxide

Reactions of acids

Q   How does dilute sulphuric acid react with magnesium?

A   When an acid reacts with a metal:

acid + metal → salt + hydrogen, therefore:

sulphuric acid + magnesium → magnesium sulphate + hydrogen

Q   What do dilute hydrochloric acid and copper carbonate react to form?

A   When an acid reacts with a carbonate:

acid + carbonate → salt + water + carbon dioxide, therefore:

hydrochloric acid + copper carbonate → copper chloride + water + carbon dioxide

Test yourself

1 Predict the word equations for:

   a) sodium burning in oxygen

   b) the combustion of zinc

   c) heating iron filings and sulphur together.

2 Predict the word equations for these reactions:

   a) hydrochloric acid and calcium carbonate   c) zinc and hydrochloric acid

   b) sulphuric acid and sodium hydroxide   d) copper oxide and nitric acid.

Check the facts

The **periodic table** and **reactivity series** enable predictions to be made.

Periodic table

This table shows that groups I–III are metals and groups IV–O are non-metals.

Q Element X has atomic number 12. What does this tell you?

A X is in group II and therefore is a metal with the physical and chemical properties of metals.

Reactivity series

The position of a metal tells us how it will react with air, water, acids (**topic 57**) and in displacement reactions (**topic 59**).

Q What happens when dilute hydrochloric acid is poured onto copper?

A No reaction. Metals below lead do not react with dilute acids.

Q What happens when magnesium is added to zinc sulphate solution?

A Zinc is displaced:

magnesium + zinc sulphate → magnesium sulphate + zinc

Test yourself

1 Element X has an atomic number of 9.
   a) Which periodic table group is it in?
   b) Is it a metal or non-metal?
   c) Will it conduct heat and electricity? Explain your answer.

2 Predict and explain what happens if a gold ring is heated in air.

3 Predict two metals that will:
   a) displace iron from iron oxide
   b) fail to displace iron from iron oxide.

4 Element A lies between zinc and iron in the reactivity series. How does it react with:
   a) water?
   b) dilute acids?
   c) magnesium sulphate solution?

Check the facts

There are three types of rock:
igneous, sedimentary, metamorphic.

Igneous rocks

- Formed whenever molten rock (magma) cools and solidifies.
- It can happen just below the Earth's crust or after a volcanic eruption.

Sedimentary rocks

- Broken and dried-out rock, dust, soil, plants, dead animals are moved about the Earth's surface by wind, rain, rivers, sea or animals.
- This material is sediment and is deposited in settled areas.
- Layers of sediment build up and, over millions of years, the weight of the top layers compacts the older lower layers into sedimentary rock.

Metamorphic rocks

- Rocks deep below the Earth's surface are under great pressure and heat.
- The pressure and heat change them to metamorphic rock.
- Both igneous and sedimentary rocks undergo this but it happens mainly to sedimentary rocks which generally lie deeper than igneous rocks.

Rocks

Test yourself

1 What is:
   a) magma?   b) sediment?

2 Describe the formation of:
   a) igneous rock   b) sedimentary rock   c) metamorphic rock.

3 Explain why there was only one type of rock present when the earth was first formed.

4 Explain why the age of fossils can be determined by where they are found in sedimentary rock.

Rocks

Check the facts

Igneous rocks

- Molten rock (magma) rises to the Earth's surface. If it stops below the surface it cools and solidifies slowly (years). It is called intrusive igneous rock and has large crystals. Granite is an example.
- When magma erupts in a volcano (lava), it cools and solidifies quickly (days/weeks). It then has small crystals and is called extrusive igneous rock. Basalt, rhyolite, pumice are examples.

Sedimentary rocks

- The composition of sedimentary rocks is determined by the original sediment.

Examples

limestone and chalk – formed from shells of dead animals

coal – from dead trees and ferns

sandstone – from sand grains

mudstone – from clay

Metamorphic rocks

- Again, composition is determined by the composition of the original.

Examples

slate – from mudstone and clay

marble – from limestone, chalk

Test yourself

1 What is lava?

2 What is the difference between intrusive and extrusive igneous rocks? Name one example of each.

3 Name two types of:
a) sedimentary and
b) metamorphic rock. Say which material each was formed from.

4 What difference would you expect to find if you examined samples of granite and basalt under a magnifying lens? Explain your answer.

www.bbc.co.uk/revision

Check the facts

Rocks are continually broken down by natural processes. This is weathering.

Physical weathering

Rocks get hot during the day and cool at night.
This causes stresses which crack, and possibly break, the rock.
These cracks fill up with rain and stream water.
This expands when it freezes, forces the rock apart and breaks it.

Chemical weathering

Acid rain, water and oxygen weather rocks by chemical reaction with minerals in the rock.

Example

Acid rain reacts with limestone (calcium carbonate).

For more on how acids react with carbonates see topic 61

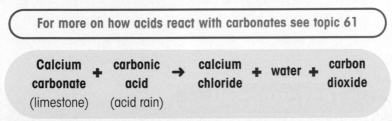

Calcium carbonate	+	carbonic acid	→	calcium chloride	+	water	+	carbon dioxide
(limestone)		(acid rain)						

Calcium chloride is soluble in water so limestone is worn away.

Biological weathering

Animals weather rocks by digging at them and walking on them.
Plants weather rocks by growing in cracks after seeds have landed.
The plant roots break up the rock.

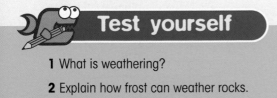

Test yourself

1 What is weathering?

2 Explain how frost can weather rocks.

3 Explain how acid rain can weather rocks.

4 Explain how desert rocks are most likely to be weathered.

5 Explain how plant life might cause pieces of rock to fall off a cliff face.

Rocks

BBC KS3 Check and Test: Science

Check the facts

All the **components** in an electric **circuit** must be connected so that an electric **current** can pass all the way round the circuit.

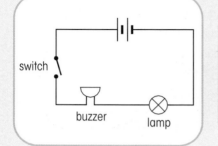

In a **series circuit** all the components are connected in one loop. The current can be turned on and off using one switch.

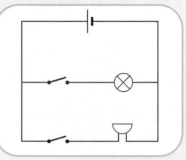

In a **parallel circuit** there are two or more branches and each branch has one or more components. The current can be controlled in each branch by separate switches.

Test yourself

1 The diagram shows a parallel circuit.
   a) Which lamps light up when switch A is pressed?
   b) Which two switches must be pressed to light lamp 4?

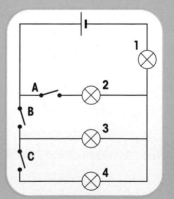

2 In the circuit below both bulbs light up.
   Suddenly both bulbs go out and bulb B is broken.

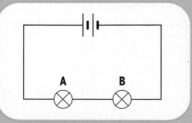

a) Bulb A is not broken so why does it go out?
b) You could connect a piece of copper wire to the circuit to make bulb A light again. Where would you put it?

Check the facts

An electric current transfers energy from a cell to the components in the rest of the circuit.

The energy in a cell comes from a chemical reaction in the cell.

Other sources of energy for an electric current include solar cells, dynamos and generators.

When an electric current passes through the **filament** in a lamp it gets hot. Because it is hot it gives out light and also warms the air around it. The brighter the lamp, the more energy is being transferred from the current.

light and heat energy

SUPERCELL

9 volt

chemical energy

When a current passes through a buzzer it **vibrates**, creating sound.

When a current passes through an electric motor, the motor turns.

Test yourself

1 Electrical devices transfer energy from an electric current to do something useful. Suggest electrical devices that do each of the following:
a) make something move
b) make a sound
c) make something warm.

2 A car battery stores energy, which is transferred around the car by an electric current. For each of these electrical devices in a car suggest what happens to the energy delivered by the electric current:
a) the heated rear window
b) the horn
c) the headlights
d) the windscreen wiper motor.

Electricity

BBC KS3 Check and Test: Science

Electricity

Check the facts

Electric current is measured using an ammeter.

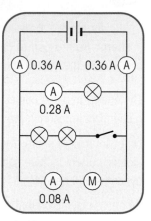

The ammeter is put in the **circuit**, in **series**, to measure the flow through the circuit.

Electric current is not used up in a circuit.

Voltage is measured with a voltmeter.

(V)

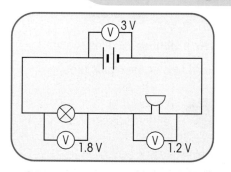

A voltmeter is placed in **parallel** in the circuit to measure the energy transfer by a device.

The voltage delivered by the power supply is equal to the voltage used by the devices in the circuit.

Test yourself

1 Copy the circuit diagram and mark on the current readings you would see on ammeters A, B and C.

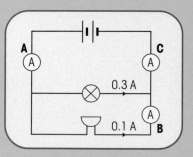

2 Copy the circuit diagram and mark on the voltage reading you would see on voltmeter D.

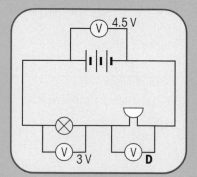

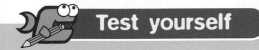

Check the facts

> The current in a series circuit depends on the components and the number of cells in the circuit.

Increasing the number of cells in a series circuit increases the current in the circuit.

Increasing the number of lamps in a series circuit decreases the available current.

Test yourself

1 Peter constructs circuit A:

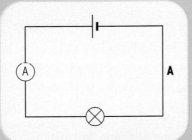

A

He wants to add a second cell to make the lamp shine more brightly.
a) Draw the circuit and add a second cell to show how the second cell should be connected to make the lamp shine more brightly.
b) How would the current through the ammeter have changed?

2 Peter now adds a second lamp to circuit A to make circuit B:

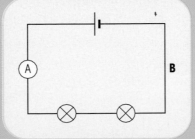

B

a) How will the brightness of the lamps in circuit B compare to the brightness in circuit A?
b) How will the reading on the ammeter in circuit B be different from the ammeter in circuit A?

Electricity

BBC KS3 Check and Test: Science

Magnetism

Check the facts

- **Magnetic** materials include iron, steel, nickel and cobalt.

- Magnets can also be made from **ceramic** materials mixed with iron.

- Magnets attract and repel other magnets.

- Magnets attract other magnetic materials.

The **north pole** of one magnet attracts the **south pole** of another magnet. Opposite poles attract.

The north pole of one magnet repels the north pole of another magnet – south poles repel each other too. Like poles repel each other.

> **A magnetic field is the space around a magnet where another magnetic field will experience a force.**

The Earth has a magnetic field. A **magnetic compass** aligns itself to point north-south in the Earth's magnetic field.

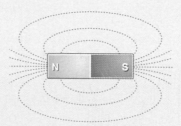

Test yourself

1 The diagram below shows two bar magnets attracted to each other. The north pole on one magnet is marked. Copy the diagram and mark the other three poles.

2 You are given three steel bars. They all look alike. Two of the bars are magnets, one is not. Describe how you can find out which one is not a magnet.

Check the facts

There is a **magnetic field** near a wire when an
electric **current** passes through the wire.

The magnetic field near a coil carrying a current is similar to the magnetic
field near a bar magnet.

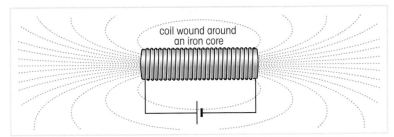

coil wound around
an iron core

The magnetic field can be made stronger by:

1 putting iron down the middle of the coil

2 putting more turns of wire in the coil

3 increasing the current running through the coil.

Test yourself

1 A student wraps a coil of wire around a wooden rod. The wire is
connected to a switch and battery. She puts three compasses near the
coil to check the field.

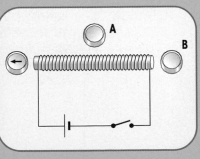

a) Copy the diagram and draw
arrows in compasses A and
B to show the direction of
the magnetic field.

b) Draw four lines on the
diagram to show the field
due to the current in the coil.

c) In which direction will the
compasses point when the switch is opened?

d) Suggest two different ways of increasing the strength of the
magnetic field.

e) What change could you make to the arrangement to reverse the
direction of the magnetic field?

Magnetism

BBC KS3 Check and Test: Science

Check the facts

> An **electromagnet** is a coil of wire, often wrapped around a piece of iron. The coil is connected to a switch and a power supply.

- An electromagnet can be switched on and off.
- There is an electromagnet in a buzzer and in an electric bell.
- An electromagnet is used to pick up steel and in relay switches to control electric circuits.
- A **reed relay** is a switch controlled by a magnet.

Test yourself

In the diagram below, the reed relay switch has two iron strips (reeds), which are close together but not touching. The strips are part of an electric circuit controlling a motor.

The strips are inside a coil of wire. The coil of wire is in a circuit supplied by a battery and controlled by switch S.

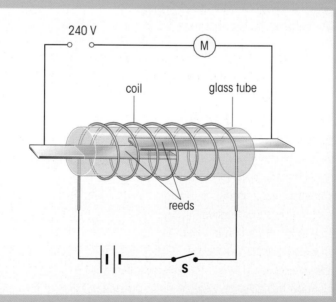

a) What happens inside the coil of wire when switch S is closed?

b) What happens to the iron strips when there is current in the wire coil?

c) Why does the motor turn when switch S is closed?

Check the facts

To measure **speed** we need to know the distance travelled and the time taken to cover the distance.

The faster something goes, the shorter the time it takes to cover the distance.

> **We measure speed in:**
> - **metres per second (m/s)**
> - **miles per hour (mph)**
> - **kilometres per hour (km/h).**

Over most journeys, the speed will vary, so we usually calculate the **average speed**:

$$\text{average speed (m/s)} = \frac{\text{distance travelled (m)}}{\text{time taken (s)}}$$

Forces and motion

Test yourself

1 In a swimming race, Paul swam 100 metres in 70 seconds, his friend Anne swam 100 metres in 65 seconds. Who swam faster?

2 A sprinter can run 100 metres in 10 seconds. What is his speed in m/s?

3 In a wheelchair race, Tanni Grey-Thompson can comfortably cover 100 metres in 20 seconds.
  a) What is her average speed in m/s?
  b) In a longer race, Tanni has an average speed of 4 m/s for 60 seconds. How far did she travel?

4 A car travels 120 miles in 3 hours.
  a) What is its average speed in mph?
  b) Why is the speed an average speed?

Forces and motion

Check the facts

> **The mass of an object tells us how much matter there is in the object.**

- Mass is measured in kilograms.

> **The weight of an object is the force of gravity on the object.**

- Weight is measured in **newtons**.

The force of gravity on the Earth pulls on everything with a force of about 10 newtons per kilogram (N/kg).

The force of gravity pulls everything towards the centre of the Earth.

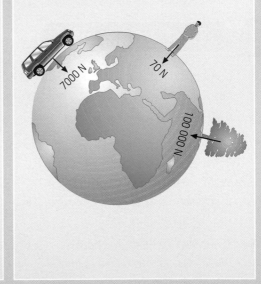

Test yourself

1 What is the unit used to measure mass?

2 What is the unit used to measure weight?

3 A load of sand has a mass of 20 kg. What is its weight?

4 In an experiment, a load of 18 newtons is suspended from a spring. What is the mass of the load?

Check the facts

On diagrams, forces are represented by arrows – the arrow tells us where the force is acting and the size of the force.

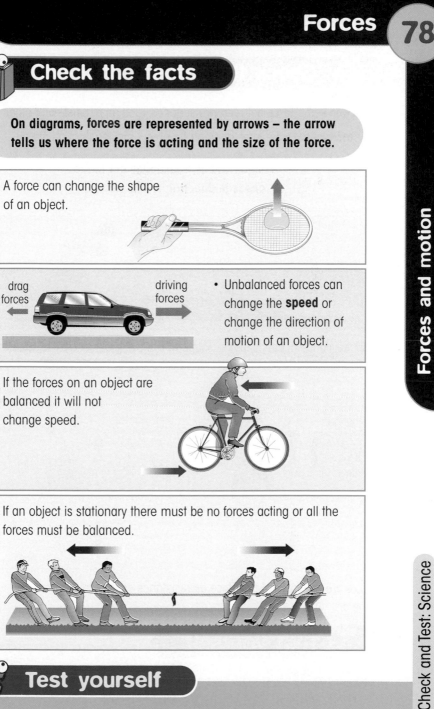

A force can change the shape of an object.

drag forces

driving forces

• Unbalanced forces can change the **speed** or change the direction of motion of an object.

If the forces on an object are balanced it will not change speed.

If an object is stationary there must be no forces acting or all the forces must be balanced.

Test yourself

1 Look at the diagram of the tennis ball. What provides the force to compress the ball?

2 Look at the diagrams of the car, the bicycle and the tug-of-war rope.
   a) Which object is accelerating? How can you tell?
   b) Which object is moving at a steady speed?
   c) What can you say about the forces on the tug of war rope?

Check the facts

Friction is the **force** between two surfaces, rubbing against each other.

Air **resistance** is the force of air on an object moving through the air.

Friction and air resistance act in the opposite direction to the motion.

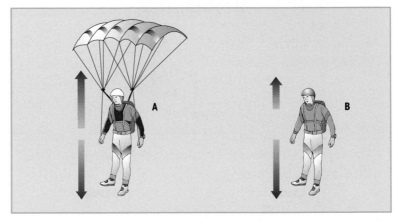

Air resistance depends on the shape of a moving object and its **speed**.

A   B

Cars are streamlined to reduce air resistance as they travel through the air.

Test yourself

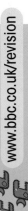

1 Look at the picture of the boy dragging the log. The log is moving at a steady speed. He is pulling the log with a force of 200 N. What is the friction force between the log and the ground?

2 Look at the two parachutists. Which parachutist is falling at a steady speed? Explain your answer.

3 Cars need friction between the tyres and the road for the car to move.
   a) Explain why a car needs this type of friction.
   b) When the road is wet, the friction between the tyres and road gets less. Explain what may happen to the car.

Check the facts

A **lever** is a simple machine that uses a **pivot** to make a task easier.

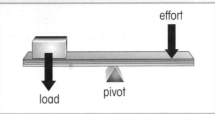

effort

load   pivot

The **force** that is applied to the lever makes the lever rotate around the pivot.

The further the force is away from the pivot the bigger the turning effect.

The turning effect of the force is called the **moment**. The moment is measured in **newton metres** (Nm)

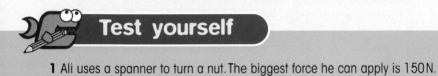

moment (Nm) = force (N) × distance from force to pivot (m)

Test yourself

1 Ali uses a spanner to turn a nut. The biggest force he can apply is 150N.

150 N

├── 0.2 m ──┤

a) Calculate the turning effect (the moment) applied to the nut.

b) How could Ali increase the turning effect of 150N?

2 Sarah is trying to open a can of paint.

She tries using a coin to lever up the edge of the lid. She cannot open it. Then she tries using the long screwdriver. Explain why it was much easier to open the can with the screwdriver.

Check the facts

> **A force acting on a small area has a bigger effect than the same force acting over a large area.**

We call this effect **pressure**. The larger the area, the smaller the pressure.

Hydraulic systems use oil to transmit pressure between places.

Test yourself

1 Explain why a sharp knife cuts through an apple more easily than a blunt knife.

2 Explain why a skier can cross the snow when a walker can't.

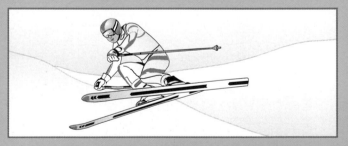

3 Explain why a small force on the brake pedal creates a large force on the brake pads.

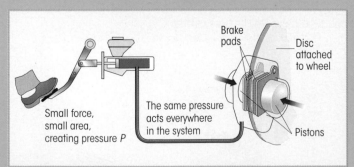

Check the facts

We calculate **pressure** using the following equation:

$$\text{pressure (N/cm}^2) = \frac{\text{force (N)}}{\text{area (cm}^2)}$$

We measure pressure in N/cm² or N/m² (also called **pascals**)

Test yourself

1 The head of a drawing pin has an area of 1 cm². The point of the drawing pin has an area of 0.01 cm². You push the pin with a force of 20 N.

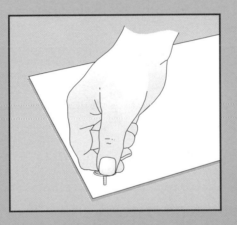

a) Calculate the pressure you exert on the drawing pin head.
b) Calculate the force the drawing pin point exerts on the board.
c) Explain why the drawing pin has a large head.

2 The total area of a skier's boots is 900 cm². The skier weighs 900 N.
   a) What is the pressure the skier exerts on the ground when he stands in his boots?
   b) The total area of his skis is 4500 cm². What is the pressure he exerts on the ground when he stands on his skis?
   c) Explain why he does not sink into the snow.

Forces and motion

BBC KS3 Check and Test: Science

Check the facts

Light spreads out from a **luminous** source, such as the hot **filament** of a lamp, the Sun or the hot gas in a fluorescent tube.

We see non-luminous objects because light from a luminous source is reflected by the object and some of this light reaches our eyes.

Light travels very fast – at 300 000 km/s. Light from the Sun takes 8.5 minutes to reach us.

Light travels in straight lines and is blocked by opaque objects, casting shadows.

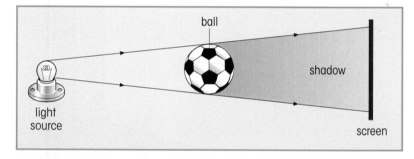

ball

shadow

light source

screen

Test yourself

1 Choose the objects that are luminous sources of light from the following list: camera, candle, lamp, mirror, the Moon, star, torch.

2 Copy the diagram of the lamp shining on the puppet.

a) Draw some rays of light from the lamp to explain how the shadow of the puppet is formed on the screen.

b) Explain what will happen to the size of the shadow if the lamp is moved closer to the puppet.

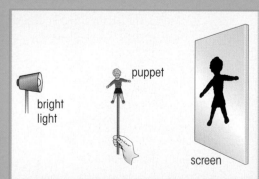

puppet

bright light

screen

Light

www.bbc.co.uk/revision

Check the facts

When light is reflected from a surface it bounces off in all directions – it is scattered.

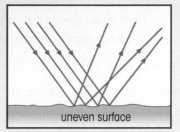

uneven surface

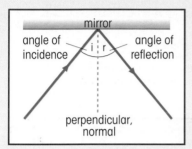

When light is reflected from a flat, shiny surface the rays are not spread out so much. More of the rays reach your eye so the surface looks bright. Shiny objects are good reflectors.

Light

When a beam of light hits a flat mirror at an angle it is always reflected off at an equal angle in the opposite direction.

Test yourself

1 A periscope uses two mirrors to change the direction of a light beam.

Complete the diagram to show the ray of light passing from the bird through the periscope to the eye. Mark an arrow on the ray to show the direction the light is travelling.

2 Look at the diagrams to show light being scattered and light being reflected from a shiny surface. Use the diagrams to explain why you can see the words on the page of a book from different places in a room, but the reflection you see in a mirror changes as you move around the room.

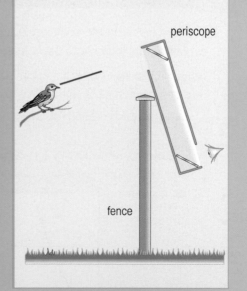

periscope

fence

BBC KS3 Check and Test: Science

Light

Check the facts

> **Light slows down when it passes into a transparent material, such as glass. As it slows down, passing from air into glass, it changes direction.**

- When the light passes back into air it speeds up and changes direction.

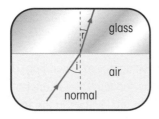
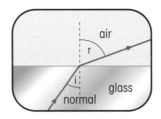

- This is called **refraction**.

Refraction can make straight things appear to bend or be broken when they are moved into water. This is because the light reflected from the object in the water enters the eye from a different direction than might be expected.

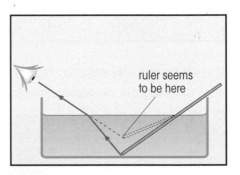

ruler seems to be here

Test yourself

1 Copy and complete the sentences using these words:
direction, refraction, slows down, speeds up.

When a ray of light travels from air into glass it _____.
This makes it change _____. When it comes back into air it _____ and changes _____ again. This is called _____.

2 In the diagrams below, light is either passing from air to glass or from glass to air. Copy the diagrams and write glass or air in the right places on the diagrams.

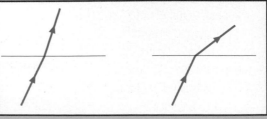

Check the facts

When white light passes through a triangular prism it is refracted and dispersed into a range of colours, which we call a spectrum.

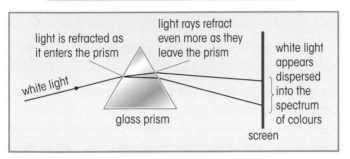

light is refracted as it enters the prism

light rays refract even more as they leave the prism

white light appears dispersed into the spectrum of colours

white light

glass prism

screen

A spectrum is seen when light is dispersed by raindrops in a rainbow.

When white light passes through a coloured filter the filter allows particular colours to pass through, the other colours are absorbed (see right).

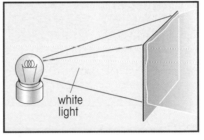

white light

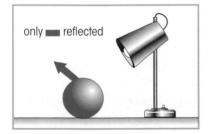

only ■ reflected

When light shines on an object some colours are reflected and others are absorbed, as shown on the left.

Test yourself

1 Copy the diagram showing white light passing into a prism.
   a) Which colour changes direction most? Mark this ray on your diagram, using the correct colour.
   b) Which colour changes direction least? Mark this ray on your diagram, using the correct colour.

2 White light passes through a red filter. What colour light emerges?

3 White light shines on a blue ball. What colour is reflected?

4 A blue ball is viewed through a red filter. What colour will be seen? Explain your answer.

Light

BBC KS3 Check and Test: Science

Check the facts

All sounds are made by vibrations.

The **pitch** of a sound tells us how high or low the sound is.

A high-pitch sound is made when something vibrates at a high **frequency**; a low-pitch sound is when something vibrates at a low frequency.

Long, thick, strings and long columns of air make low-pitch sounds. Tightening a string or shortening the column of air will raise the pitch.

The loudness of a sound depends on how big the vibrations are – large vibrations make loud sounds.

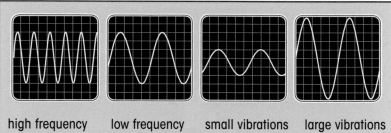

| high frequency | low frequency | small vibrations | large vibrations |
| high pitch | low pitch | quiet | loud |

Test yourself

1 Look at the picture of a guitar and then copy and complete the sentences using some of these words: **high, higher, low, lower, vibrate**.

The strings on a guitar _____ to make a sound. The thick strings will make a _____-pitch note. If the string is tightened the pitch of the note will become _____. If the string is shortened the note will become _____. High-pitch notes are made when the strings _____ at a _____ frequency.

Sound

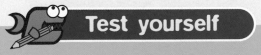

Check the facts

The vibrations that make a sound are passed through the air by making particles in the air vibrate. This is a sound wave.

The vibrations pass through our ear to a nerve, which sends a message to the brain – that is how we hear the sound.

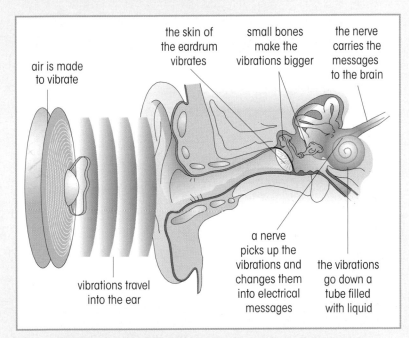

the skin of the eardrum vibrates

small bones make the vibrations bigger

the nerve carries the messages to the brain

air is made to vibrate

vibrations travel into the ear

a nerve picks up the vibrations and changes them into electrical messages

the vibrations go down a tube filled with liquid

Loud sounds cause large vibrations in the ear – this can cause damage and temporary deafness.

As people get older they cannot hear high **frequency** sounds so well.

Test yourself

1 Make a list of the parts of the ear, putting them in the order that they vibrate when the sound reaches the ear.

2 Suggest why it is important for people working with loud machines to wear ear-defenders.

Sound

BBC KS3 Check and Test: Science

Check the facts

Sound needs particles to pass on the **vibrations**. Sound can't travel through empty space.

Light can travel through empty space (a **vacuum**).

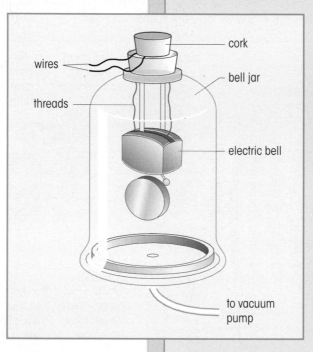

- cork
- wires
- bell jar
- threads
- electric bell
- to vacuum pump

Sound travels more quickly through **dense** solids.

Sound is absorbed by some materials.

Light travels at 300 000 km/s. Sound travels at 330 m/s. This is why lightening is seen before thunder is heard in a thunderstorm.

Light and sound both spread out from their source. The further away you are from the source, the dimmer the light and the quieter the sound.

Test yourself

1 Look at the picture of the bell in the bell jar. The air is pumped out of the jar. Explain why you cannot hear the bell but you can still see it.

2 Describe how a firework can be used to show that light travels much faster than sound.

Sound

www.bbc.co.uk/revision

Check the facts

The Sun appears to move across the sky each day, rising in the east and setting in the west.

The Sun rises higher in the sky in summer than in winter.

The Moon appears to move across the sky each night and to change shape during a month.

Stars appear to move around the sky each night.

> **The Earth is spinning on its axis, making one rotation every day – this is why the Sun, Moon and stars appear to move across the sky.**

The Moon travels in orbit around the Earth. It makes one compete **orbit** in 28 days.

We see the Moon when light from the Sun is reflected from the surface of the Moon.

The Earth is in orbit around the Sun. It makes one complete orbit each year.

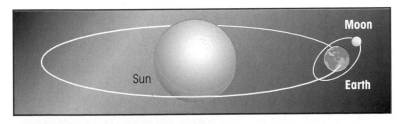

Moon
Sun
Earth

Test yourself

1 Copy and complete the drawings to show how the Moon changes during a month.

2 Describe how the length of a day (from sunrise to sunset) changes during a year, starting in January.

Earth in space

Check the facts

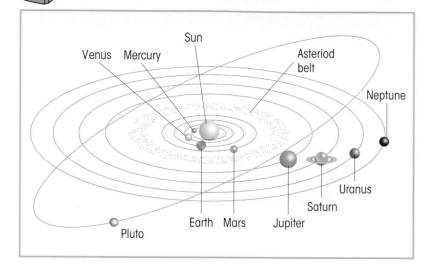

The Earth is one of nine planets in orbit around the Sun.

> **The planets are held in orbit by the gravitational attraction between the Sun and the planets.**

Some of the planets, including the Earth, have moons in orbit around them. These moons are held in orbit by the gravitational attraction between the planet and its moon(s).

The larger the orbit of a planet, the longer it takes for the planet to complete one orbit.

The Sun is a star. It is the source of light by which we see the moon and other planets.

The other stars in the sky are much further away than the Sun and planets.

Test yourself

1 Which planet is furthest from the Sun?

2 Which planet will take the shortest time to complete one orbit?

3 Copy and complete the sentences:

There are _____ planets in the Solar System, all orbiting the

_____ . They are held in orbit by the force of _____ .

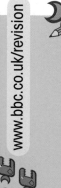

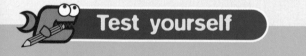

Check the facts

Rockets are used to take **satellites** up into **orbit** around the Earth.

Satellites are held in orbit by the force of gravity.

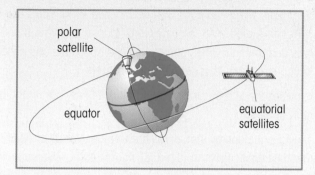

polar
satellite

equator

equatorial
satellites

Some satellites are used to transmit television and radio signals around the Earth.

Some satellites are used to collect information about the Earth and some satellites have detectors pointing away from the Earth to collect information about the rest of the Universe.

Rockets are also used to send **probes** out into the Solar System. The probe will use the pull of gravity from some of the planets to move itself.

Test yourself

1 Write down three uses of satellites.

2 What is the force that keeps all the satellites in orbit?

3 Look at the picture of the satellites in orbit. Which satellite will be moving more quickly? Give a reason for your answer.

BBC KS3 Check and Test: Science

Energy resources

Check the facts

The Sun is the key source of energy for life on Earth – plants need light to grow, animals need plants for food.

In the distant past, energy from the Sun was locked up in plants and tiny animals. When they died, their remains were trapped under mud and sand. These plants and animals were compressed over the years and changed to become oil, coal and gas. These are the **fossil fuels**.

The Sun provides the energy for **photosynthesis**. Plants lock up the energy of the Sun in **glucose**.

The Sun provides the energy that drives the weather. Winds are due to temperature differences across the planet. Rain is part of the water cycle, driven by energy from the Sun.

Test yourself

1 Write down three ways in which the Sun is essential for humans to live.

2 In many parts of the world wood is an important energy source. Why can trees be described as a way of storing energy from the Sun?

3 Explain how energy from the Sun is important in driving the water cycle.

Check the facts

Fossil fuels – coal, oil and natural gas took millions of years to be formed and cannot be replaced. They are non-renewable energy sources.

Wind, waves, running water and sunlight are energy sources driven by the Sun. They are always present and are renewable energy sources.

Wood and other plant materials are used as energy sources – including for heating and to make fuel for cars. Plant material used in this way is called **biomass**. As plants are cut down and used, new plants grow in their place. So biomass is a renewable energy source.

The tides are driven by the gravitational attraction of the Moon. The moving water of the tides is another renewable energy source.

Energy from the Sun is trapped by solar panels on the roofs of houses and is used to heat water; energy from the Sun is also trapped by **solar cells** and used to generate electricity, which is often stored in batteries.

Deep underground, rocks are hot. Water pumped into the rocks becomes healed and is used to heat houses. This is **geothermal** energy.

Test yourself

1 Complete this table, trying to put at least one energy source in each box.

	renewable energy source	non-renewable energy source
energy comes directly from the Sun		
energy comes indirectly from the Sun		
energy does not originally come from the Sun		

Check the facts

Most electricity is generated by using a **turbine** to drive a **spinning coil**. The turbine might be turned by:

- high-pressure steam produced by heating water (by burning a **fossil fuel** or waste material, or in a **nuclear reactor**)

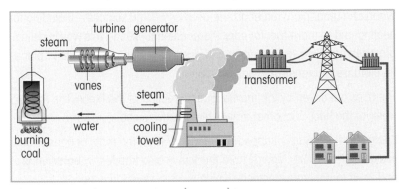

- moving water (the moving water might be waves on the sea, the tide, water running down from a high-storage dam – **hydroelectric power**)

- the wind.

Some electricity is generated in solar cells and stored in batteries for local use.

Most electricity in the UK is generated by burning fossil fuels, which have a limited life and produce **carbon dioxide**, which contributes to **global warming**.

Many people believe that we need to reduce the amount of electricity we use, to reduce the use of fossil fuels.

Test yourself

1 Name a renewable source of energy can be used to generate electricity.

2 Write down two reasons why we should try to use alternatives to fossil fuels to generate electricity.

3 Which renewable source of energy might be best to generate electricity where you live? Give your reasons.

Energy resources

www.bbc.co.uk/revision

Check the facts

Batteries store energy using chemicals. When the battery is connected to a **circuit** a chemical reaction releases energy to the electric **current**.

Hydroelectric dams store water high up in the hills. When the demand for electricity is high the water is released to turn **turbines**.

Plants store energy, which can be released by burning. The heat may be used for cooking or for generating electricity. The plants are also used as food to supply energy to animals.

Energy may be transported around the country in petrol tankers or coal trains, but the most effective way of transferring energy from one place to another is through the **electric grid system**.

Test yourself

1 Explain why solar energy might be stored in batteries before use.

2 Batteries are an expensive way of supplying electricity. Suggest two situations where you might use batteries rather than mains electricity.

3 Explain why it is better to generate electricity close to where the coal is found, rather than build a power station near each town.

Energy resources

Energy transfer

Check the facts

When a material is heated, energy is transferred into the material and the particles move around more and the temperature rises.

> **Temperature is measured using a thermometer; the unit for temperature is degrees Celsius (˚C). Energy is measured in joules (J).**

When there is a temperature difference between an object and its surroundings, energy will flow from the high temperature to the low temperature. The warm object will get cooler and the surroundings will warm up.

Water needs a lot of energy to raise its temperature by just one degree. Metals need much less energy to raise their temperature by the same amount.

A large **mass** needs more energy to raise its temperature than a small mass of the same material.

Test yourself

1 Complete these sentences:

Temperature is measured in _____; it tells us how

_____ something is. Heat energy is measured in

_____; it tells us how much energy is needed to warm something up.

2 Use your ideas about temperature and energy to describe what happens when:
a) a hot cup of tea is placed in a cold room
b) an ice lolly is left on the kitchen table.

Check the facts

Energy is transferred when there is a temperature difference between two things.

Energy is transferred from the hotter part of a solid to the colder part by the particles in the material. Particles in the hot part vibrate more. These **vibrations** are passed on to the cooler particles next to them, which also begin to vibrate. Energy spreads through the material until it is all at the same temperature. This is called **conduction**.

Metals are good **conductors**. Most non-metals are poor conductors. Most liquids and gases are poor conductors. Poor conductors are used as **insulators**.

When a liquid or gas becomes warm it expands and becomes less **dense**. The warm liquid or gas rises above the cooler fluid, which sinks. This flow of warm fluid is called **convection current**.

Particles at the surface of a liquid may have enough energy to leave the liquid to become a **vapour**. This is **evaporation**. The particles that leave the liquid take away their energy with them, leaving the liquid cooler.

Test yourself

1 Use your ideas about conduction, convection and evaporation to explain why:
   a) bubble wrap is used to line a greenhouse in winter
   b) the element is placed at the bottom of electric kettles
   c) sweating helps us to keep cool.

Energy transfer

BBC KS3 Check and Test: Science

Energy transfer

Check the facts

> **Warm bodies lose energy by infrared radiation; the hotter the body the more energy is radiated.**

Infrared radiation travels in waves that travel at the same speed as light.

Infrared radiation can travel through a **vacuum**. The warmth of the Sun reaches the Earth by radiation through space.

Dark-coloured objects emit and absorb radiation better than light-coloured objects.

Test yourself

1 Explain why it will be much warmer inside a black car on a hot sunny day, than inside a white car.

2 Suggest cooking methods that use each of: conduction, convection and radiation.

3 Suggest why it might be better if central heating radiators in houses were called convectors, rather than radiators.

Check the facts

Whenever energy is used to do a job, the total amount of energy remains the same.

During an energy transfer some energy is lost to the surroundings.

> **The energy lost to the surroundings warms up the surroundings slightly; it is difficult to get that energy back. This energy is not destroyed but it is wasted.**

Energy-efficient devices lose as little energy as possible.

Test yourself

1 Look at the picture of the energy transfers that take place in a car.

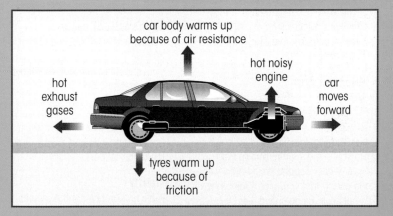

car body warms up because of air resistance

hot noisy engine

hot exhaust gases

car moves forward

tyres warm up because of friction

a) Where does the energy come from to drive the engine?

b) Only about one quarter of the energy supplied to the car is transferred to the moving car. What happens to the rest?

2 Suggest two changes you could make to your life to use energy more efficiently.

Energy transfer

Answers

1 The parts of cells
1 The cell wall.
2 No cell wall, vacuole or chloroplast.
3 Nucleus, cytoplasm, cell membrane.
4 Potato cells wouldn't have chloroplasts.

2 How cells work
1 The nucleus.
2 Make food by photosynthesis.
3 It would lose support and wilt.
4 The nucleus.
5 In the vacuole.

3 Special cells
1 1:D, 2:A, 3:B, 4:C.

4 Food
1 Protein; fish and meat.
2 Fat
3 a) Carbohydrate b) protein c) fat.
4 Because we use it to release energy.
5 It contains the five food classes (protein, carbohydrates, fat, minerals and vitamins).

5 A balanced diet
1 Fat
2 For more energy.
3 They couldn't get supplies of fresh fruit and vegetables with vitamin C.
4 Starvation means that you do not have enough food to provide you with the energy that you need. Malnutrition is not having a balanced diet.

6 The principles of digestion
1 It is broken down.
2 To make it soluble so that it can pass into the blood.
3 Enzymes
4 Digestive enzymes
5 In the mouth.

7 Blood
1 They carry oxygen.
2 Digested foods, vitamins, minerals, hormones.
3 It transports urea to the kidneys and carbon dioxide to the lungs.
4 White blood cells kill invading disease-causing microbes and platelets help blood to form a clot, which acts as a barrier against invasion by microbes.

8 The skeleton
1 Protection, movement, support.
2 Joints
3 A ball-and-socket joint allows multi-directional movement but a hinge joint can only move in one plane.

9 Muscle and movement
1 a) They hold bones in place.
  b) They join muscles to bone.
2 The biceps – it bends the arm.
3 Muscles cannot lengthen. One pulls one way; the other pulling back.
4 Animals must move in search of their food and must escape danger.

10 Human reproduction
1 In the ovaries.
2 One
3 In the oviduct.

11 The menstrual cycle
1 It becomes richly supplied with blood.
2 28 days.
3 It passes out of the vagina with the lining of the womb.

12 Pregnancy
1 It contains a liquid which protects the embryo from jolts and bumps.
2 The umbilical cord.

13 Puberty
1 Pubic hair and hair in the armpits. Increase in growth rate.
2 a) 13
  b) 14
3 The shoulders broaden and the voice box grows bigger. Pubic hair grows. Hair grows in the armpits. The penis and testes grow larger.

14 The breathing system
1 a) Oxygen
  b) Carbon dioxide
2 Moist, thin single-celled wall, large surface area richly supplied with blood.
3 Diffusion

15 The effects of smoking
1 Bronchitis, emphysema, cancer.
2 The tubes leading to the lungs have hair-like cilia that trap dust and stop particles reaching the air-sacs. The nicotine in tobacco stops cilia working.

3 Cancer

4 Tobacco smoke can be inhaled by anyone who is near a smoker and cause lung diseases.

16 Respiration

1 Respiration is the chemical release of energy from glucose. Breathing is the physical exchange of gases at a breathing surface, by diffusion.

2 In all living cells.

3 Aerobic respiration uses oxygen, releasing more energy than anaerobic respiration.

4 Gills (fish) or skin (frogs).

17 How gases are carried

1 Haemoglobin

2 The random movement of particles, resulting in a net movement from high to low concentration.

3 Oxygen + Haemoglobin → Oxyhaemoglobin

4 a) There is more oxygen in air breathed in than in air breathed out.
b) There is less carbon dioxide in air breathed in than in air breathed out.

18 Effects of drugs

1 Alcohol slows down reactions.

2 A chemical which alters behaviour and chemical reactions in the body.

3 Addiction is when someone is so dependent on a drug that their health and behaviour are affected if the drug is not available.

4 The nervous system.

19 Immunity

1 White blood cells.

2 Antibodies

3 A disease-causing microbe.

4 Chickenpox

20 Immunisation

1 a) Tuberculosis, rubella, polio
b) Whooping cough, cholera

2 Smallpox

3 An antibody.

21 Photosynthesis

1 Water, carbon dioxide, chlorophyll.

2 Light energy to chemical energy.

3 a) water b) carbon dioxide

22 Plant growth

1 Leaf, stem or root.

2 It has to divide.

3 In buds; at the tip of the stem; at the tip of the root.

4 Photosynthesis

23 Plant growth and soil

1 To grow.

2 Nitrates, phosphates or sulphates.

3 The water displaces oxygen, which is needed for respiration in root cells.

4 Decaying animal and plant material.

24 Variation and the environment

1 Inheritance and environment.

2 Breed between themselves and have young which are capable of breeding.

3 Surroundings in which organisms live

4 The mule cannot reproduce but the dog can.

25 Variation and inheritance

1 Genetics

2 Genes

3 Faulty genes

4 The fusion of an egg with a sperm.

26 Selective breeding

1 Grasses

2 Variation

3 Wool, milk production, meat production

27 The principles of classification

1 5

2 Primates

3 A backbone.

4 Apes

28 The main groups of plants

1 Mosses

2 Chlorophyll

3 Flowering plants

29 The main groups of animals

1 a) mammals b) amphibians
c) reptiles

2 Reptiles

30 Adaptation

1 Adapted for eating different foods.
2 For camouflage.
3 Light, hollow bones
4 They reduce the amount of water loss in the heat of the day.

31 Competition

1 Lions' manes, stags' antlers, bright colours of male tropical fish.
2 Minerals; water
3 When more offspring are produced than could possibly survive.
4 Survival of the best able to breed.

32 Food webs

1 The direction of the flow of energy.
2 They are the only organisms that can make their own food.
3 The foxes would eat more of his sheep and chickens.

33 Food pyramids

1 One tenth.
2 Heat, excreted materials.
3 They would get fewer.

34 Microbes

1 Disease-causing microbes.
2 Cholera, typhoid, tuberculosis, food poisoning.
3 Bread, yoghurt, cheese.
4 Bacteria recycle essential elements, such as carbon and nitrogen.

35 Solids, liquids and gases

1 Solid, liquid, gas.
2 Solid turning to liquid.
3 Liquid turning to gas (or vapour).
4 The temperature at which the solid has completely turned to liquid.
5 The amount of matter packed into a space. Density $(g/cm^3) =$ mass (g) / volume (cm^3)
6 Density = mass / volume density of $X = 8/6 = 1.33 \ g/cm^3$

36 Particles

1 a) gas; b) liquid; c) solid; d) solid; e) solid; f) gas
2 a) Particles shaking but staying in the same place.
   b) Moving around without a pattern or system.

c) Forces between particles

37 Properties of solids, liquids, gases

1 a) Because particles are fixed in place.
   b) Because particles move in all directions and spread completely throughout a container.
   c) Because particles are able to move from place to place.
   d) Inter-particle forces are strong enough to stop particles escaping.
2 The spread of gas particles to completely fill a container.
3 Solid to liquid; liquid to gas; gas to liquid; liquid to solid.
4 Heating gives energy to the particles, and they hit the sides of their container harder, therefore exerting greater pressure.

38 Physical changes

1 One in which no new substance is formed and which can easily be reversed by changing the conditions.
2 Any two examples but two changes of state are the most likely answers.
3 35 g salt, because 135 g solution minus 100 g water equals 35 g salt.
4 a) stirring sugar in water
   d) melting iron
   e) painting a wall
   f) folding paper
   Because each of these can easily be reversed and no new substances are formed in each case.

39 Energy in changes of state

1 Because particles use heat energy to overcome the forces holding them in the liquid and thus escape to become gas/vapour at 100°C.
2 Because the heat originally used to change the solid to liquid is released when the liquid changes back to solid.
3 Because heat has to be taken in to be used as energy, allowing the particles to break out of the rigid solid structure and become liquid in which the particles can flow.
4 Nail varnish remover particles use the skin's heat energy to evaporate.

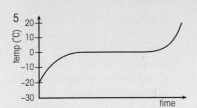

40 Solutions

1 a) The material that dissolves.
   b) The liquid in which the solute dissolves.
   c) A solution containing a small amount of solute.
   d) A solution containing a large amount of solute.
   e) Solution that no more solute can dissolve in because the solution is 'full'.
   f) A material which dissolves in water is soluble.
   g) A material which does not dissolve in water is insoluble.
2 Evaporate some water by heating or leaving it out in the air for some time.
3 a, c, e

41 Solubility and solvents

1 Water, ethanol, white spirit, paraffin are mentioned in the text.
2 No, because grease doesn't dissolve in water.
3 The maximum amount of a solute (g) that will dissolve in 100g of the solvent at a particular temperature.

4

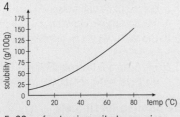

5 32 g of potassium nitrate are given out of the solution (65g at 40°C minus 33 g at 20°C).

42 Elements

1 A single material that cannot be broken down into anything simpler.
2 The smallest part of an element that can exist.
3 a) Na b) H c) Ca d) Fe
4 a) zinc b) oxygen c) copper
   d) potassium
5 hydrogen and oxygen

6 a) sodium, chlorine
   b) calcium, carbon, oxygen
   c) calcium, oxygen, hydrogen
   d) hydrogen, sulphur, oxygen
   e) sodium, oxygen, hydrogen
   f) hydrogen, nitrogen, oxygen

43 The periodic table

1 Protons, neutrons, electrons
2 The number of protons in atoms of the element.
3 a) lithium Li, sodium Na, potassium K
   b) carbon C, silicon Si
   c) fluorine F, chlorine Cl
4 a) lithium Li or potassium K
   b) beryllium Be or calcium Ca
   c) fluorine F
   d) helium He or argon Ar
5 a) 13 b) 9 c) 20 d) 6

44 Compounds

1 A pure material made up of two or more elements combined together.
2 Any four compounds are acceptable – most answers will give four of the six listed in the table given in the text.
3 The smallest part of compound made up of two or more atoms combined.
4 a) zinc, oxygen
   b) calcium, chlorine
   c) lead, sulphur
   d) potassium, iodine
   e) calcium, bromine
   f) magnesium, carbon, oxygen

45 Formulae

1 a) H_2O b) H_2SO_4 c) NaCl d) NH_3
2 a) one carbon, two oxygen
   b) one magnesium, one oxygen
   c) one sodium, one chlorine

Name	Number of each atom
Aluminium oxide	1 aluminium, 3 oxygen
Calcium chloride	1 calcium, 2 chlorine
Zinc sulphate	1 zinc, 1 sulphur, 4 oxygen

4 The law states that the composition of any one compound is fixed.

46 Mixtures

1 A substance containing two or more materials that are jumbled together but not chemically combined.

Answers

2 Mixtures: pizza, air, petrol, toothpaste, tap water, lipstick.
Pure elements: oxygen, aluminium.
Pure compound: steam.

3 The four differences contained in the table in the text should be listed.

47 Separating mixtures

1 a) An undissolved solid and a liquid.
b) A soluble solid and a liquid.
c) A mixture of coloured liquids.

2 a) The liquid collected after filtration.
b) The solid collected after filtration.
c) To boil away the solvent from a solution, leaving the solute behind.

3 Evaporation produces the solute from a solution. Distillation produces the solvent from a solution.

4 Crush the rock salt; stir the crushed rock salt in water; filter; evaporate the filtrate, which is a solution of pure salt, until the pure salt remains.

48 Chemical reactions

1 a) A material that takes part in a chemical reaction.
b) A material produced as a result of a chemical reaction.
c) In any chemical reaction, the total mass of the products equals the total mass of reactants.

2 New materials are produced; cannot easily be reversed.

3 Because new materials are produced and the changes cannot be reversed.

4 The law of conservation of mass explains that the same atoms are used throughout a reaction; atoms cannot be made or lost; therefore mass must remain constant.

5 2.0 g magnesium oxide minus 1.2 g magnesium equals 0.8 g oxygen used.

49 Word equations

1 a) hydrogen + oxygen ⟶ water
b) sodium + oxygen ⟶ sodium oxide
c) calcium oxide + water ⟶ calcium hydroxide
d) sulphuric acid + magnesium ⟶ magnesium sulphate + hydrogen

2 a) hydrochloric acid, calcium carbonate
b) calcium chloride, water, carbon dioxide

c) hydrochloric acid + calcium carbonate ⟶ calcium chloride + water + carbon dioxide

3 a) sodium chloride
b) hydrochloric, hydrogen
c) potassium sulphate
d) oxygen

50 Chemistry in living systems

1 Enzymes break down food into single molecules by chemical reaction; without this process food cannot enter the bloodstream.

2 Photosynthesis: energy from sun converts carbon dioxide from atmosphere and water from soil to glucose, once they have been absorbed by chlorophyll in leaves.

carbon dioxide *chlorophyll* glucose
+ ⟶ +
water *sunlight* oxygen

3 The process by which digested food and oxygen react together in the bloodstream to produce energy.

food carbon dioxide
+ ⟶ +
oxygen water + energy

4 No. Breathing is how the body takes in oxygen; respiration combines this oxygen with food to produce energy.

51 Chemistry in everyday life

1 Plastics, glass, fibres, ceramics, metals.
2 Any acceptable answers.
3 Keeps out air and water.
4 Any acceptable answers.
5 The skin prevents air reaching the apple itself.
6 The bottom is in contact with moisture in the soil as well as the air.

52 Burning fossil fuels

1 a) A material burned to produce heat.
b) Fuels formed over millions of years from decaying plant and animal remains.
c) The presence of unwanted materials in the air.

2 Two of: coal, gas, oil.

3 Acid gases, such as carbon dioxide, sulphur dioxide, nitrogen dioxide, dissolving in rain to form acids; any acceptable answers from the text.

4 Any acceptable answers based upon no emissions.

Answers

5 Wind and air currents move the acid rain to non-industrial areas.

6 Any acceptable answers based on sources of energy, such as sun, wind, waves that cannot be used up.

53 The greenhouse effect

1 carbon dioxide, sulphur dioxide, nitrogen dioxide, methane

2 Heavy gases remain in the atmosphere and trap heat in.

3 Any acceptable answers based upon the reasons given in the text.

4 Methane is produced from rotting waste and sewage; our society is producing more and more of this.

5 Any acceptable answers based on using less wood of the big rainforests.

54 Metals

1 a) Can be beaten into shapes.
   b) Can be stretched into wires.
   c) Allows electricity to flow through itself.
   d) Allows heat to flow through itself.

2 mercury

3 a) no b) no c) yes

4 a) Malleable, conductor of heat.
   b) Ductile, conductor of electricity.
   c) Malleable, conductor of heat.
   d) Light, shiny.

55 Non-metals

1 a) graphite (carbon) b) bromine
   c) one of sulphur, carbon, phosphorus
   d) diamond (carbon)

2 Check against lists on p 59 and p 60.

3 a) metal b) metal c) non-metal
   d) non-metal

56 Metals reacting with air/water

1 a) sodium + oxygen → sodium oxide
   b) magnesium + oxygen → magnesium oxide
   c) potassium + oxygen → potassium oxide
   d) sodium + water → sodium hydroxide + hydrogen
   e) zinc + steam → zinc oxide + hydrogen
   f) magnesium + steam → magnesium oxide + hydrogen
   g) potassium + water → potassium hydroxide + hydrogen

2 a) metal + oxygen → metal oxide
   b) metal + water → metal hydroxide + hydrogen
   c) metal + steam → metal oxide + hydrogen

57 Metals reacting with acids

1 A compound formed when the hydrogen of an acid is replaced by a metal; any acceptable example. One element pushes another element out of a compound, taking its place; any acceptable example.

2 a) magnesium + hydrochloric acid → magnesium chloride + hydrogen
   b) magnesium + sulphuric acid → magnesium sulphate + hydrogen
   c) zinc + hydrochloric acid → zinc chloride + hydrogen
   d) zinc + sulphuric acid → zinc sulphate + hydrogen

3 a) aluminium sulphate
   b) calcium chloride
   c) iron chloride
   d) magnesium nitrate

58 Reactivity series

1 The metals placed in order of reactivity (the most reactive at the top).

2 a) potassium; gold b) silver, gold
   c) aluminium, zinc, iron
   d) Three of calcium, magnesium, aluminium, zinc, iron.
   e) Two of aluminium, zinc, iron.

59 Displacement of metals

1 a) magnesium oxide, zinc
   b) copper oxide, zinc
   c) magnesium, iron oxide
   d) magnesium chloride, copper
   e) lead, iron nitrate.

2 a) lead + supper sulphate → lead sulphate + copper
   b) magnesium + lead nitrate → magnesium nitrate + lead
   c) no reaction
   d) zinc + lead oxide → zinc oxide + lead
   e) magnesium + aluminium sulphate → magnesium sulphate + aluminium
   f) no reaction
   g) no reaction

h) magnesium + aluminium oxide → magnesium oxide + aluminium

i) copper + silver nitrate → copper nitrate + silver

j) no reaction

60 Acids

1 hydrochloric, sulphuric, nitric acids

2 carbonic acid, ethanoic acid are the two in the text; others (e.g. citric acid) are acceptable.

3 Material that changes colour to show whether a solution is acid or not.

4 red

5 a) 0–3
   b) 4–6, but low ranges for strong acids and towards 7 for weak acids are acceptable.

6 Answers around 4–6 are acceptable; lemon juice must be a weak acid because we can drink it with no harm.

61 Reactions of acids

1 a) chlorides   b) nitrates

2 a) hydrochloric acid + copper oxide (or copper hydroxide) → copper chloride + water
   b) sulphuric acid + zinc oxide (or zinc hydroxide) → zinc sulphate + water

3 a) potassium carbonate + nitric acid → potassium nitrate + water + carbon dioxide
   b) magnesium carbonate + sulphuric acid → magnesium sulphate + water + carbon dioxide

4 a) iron + sulphuric acid → iron sulphate + hydrogen
   b) magnesium + hydrochloric acid → magnesium chloride + hydrogen

62 Alkalis

1 A material that reacts with acids to produce a salt and water; bases are oxides and hydroxides; any two named oxides or hydroxides of metals, e.g. copper oxide, magnesium hydroxide, are acceptable.

2 A soluble base; sodium hydroxide and potassium hydroxide are in the text but any of the oxides or hydroxides of sodium, potassium, calcium, ammonium are acceptable.

3 Turn it blue.

4 a) High pH ranges, e.g. 13 or 14.
   b) pH ranges towards 7, e.g. 8–10.

5 A solution of pH 7.

6 About pH 8–10; it must be a weak alkali as it does us no harm if eaten.

7 Answers relating to danger; care; keep away from children; do not eat are acceptable.

63 Neutralisation

1 The reaction between acid and alkali; because the product is pH 7 (neutral)

2 a) sulphuric acid + sodium hydroxide → sodium sulphate + water
   b) nitric acid + potassium hydroxide → potassium nitrate + water

3 a) lime b) peat

4 To neutralise the excess acid in the stomach.

5 ammonia + sulphuric acid → ammonium sulphate
   ammonia + nitric acid → ammonium nitrate

64 Chemical reactions

1 a) sodium + oxygen → sodium oxide
   b) zinc + oxygen → zinc oxide
   c) iron + sulphur → iron sulphide

2 a) hydrochloric acid + calcium carbonate → calcium chloride + water + carbon dioxide
   b) sulphuric acid + sodium hydroxide → sodium sulphate + water
   c) zinc + hydrochloric acid → zinc chloride + hydrogen
   d) copper oxide + nitric acid → copper nitrate + water

65 Table of elements

1 a) VII
   b) non-metal
   c) No, because non-metals don't conduct either heat or electricity.

2 Nothing will happen/no reaction will take place. Gold is at the bottom of the reactivity series and does not react with air at all.

3 a) Any two metals above iron in the reactivity series.

b) Any two metals below iron in the reactivity series.

4 a) Reacts with steam to give its oxide + hydrogen.

b) Reacts to form hydrogen and its salt of the acid.

c) No reaction. It will not displace magnesium because it is below magnesium in the reactivity series.

66 Formation of rocks

1 a) Molten rock.

b) Deposited particles of rock, soil, etc.

2 a) Cooling and solidifying molten rock

b) Lower layers of sediment compacted into rock by pressure of upper layers.

c) Heat and pressure on igneous or sedimentary rocks that are deep below the earth's surface.

3 First rocks formed by cooling of molten material; so only igneous rocks could have been present at first.

4 In sedimentary rocks, lower layers are oldest; so knowing the layer in which a fossil was found indicates age.

67 Composition of rocks

1 Magma erupting from a volcano.

2 Intrusive rocks formed by slow cooling of lava below earth's surface, e.g. granite; extrusive rocks formed by quick cooling of lava above the earth's surface, e.g. basalt/rhyolite/pumice.

3 Examples from the text usually given.

4 Granite – large crystals – intrusive igneous rock – cooled slowly.
Basalt – small crystals – extrusive igneous rock – cooled quickly.

68 Weathering of rocks

1 Rocks broken down by natural processes.

2 Rain in cracks – freezes at night – expands when solid ice – forces cracks apart

3 Undergoes chemical reactions with the materials in the rock.

4 Physical weathering (heat and cold alternately during day and night) this expansion and contraction produces stresses which crack, breaking the rock.

5 Plant roots burrow into rock causing it to break off.

69 Electric circuits

1 a) 1 and 2 (b) B and C

2 a) The circuit between the lamp and the battery is broken.

b)

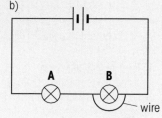

70 Energy in electrical circuits

1 a) motor b) loudspeaker c)heater

2 a) Warms glass and surroundngs.

b) Makes sound waves.

c) Produces light and becomes warm.

d) Moves wipers and becomes warm.

71 Measuring current and voltage

1 A = 0.4 A; B = 0.1 A; C = 0.4 A

2 D = 1.5 V

72 Current in electrical circuits

1 a)

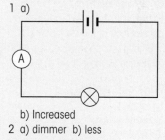

b) Increased

2 a) dimmer b) less

73 Magnetic fields

1

2 Like poles of magnets repel each other, so find the two ends which repel each other these two bars are the magnets.

Answers

74 Making an electromagnet

1 a) and b)

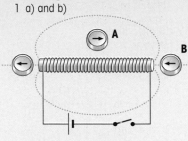

c) Towards magnetic north
d) Increase the number of turns or batteries in the circuit; use a steel rod instead of a wooden one.
e) Reverse the battery

75 Using an electromagnet

1 a) There is a magnetic field
b) They move closer together
c) The coil's current makes the strips touch, completing the motor circuit.

76 Speed, distance and time

1 Anne
2 10 m/s
3 a) 5 m/s   b) 240 m
4 a) 40 miles per hour
b) Because the speed varies - some acceleration at the start, probably speeding up and slowing down in the traffic and slowing down at the end.

77 Mass and weight

1 Kilogram
2 Newton
3 200 N
4 1.8 kg

78 Forces

1 The hand holding the tennis racket
2 a) car, bigger force forwards
b) cyclist, forces balanced
c) forces balanced, rope stationary

79 Friction

1 200 N
2 A. Forces are equal and opposite.
3 a) Friction between tyre and road drives car forwards, otherwise wheel would spin.
b) It is more likely to skid, less control.

80 Turning forces

1 a) Moment = force x distance to pivot
= 150 N x 0.2 m = 30 N m
b) Move his hand to the end of the spanner
2 The screwdriver lets Sarah exert a force further from the pivot, giving a bigger turning effect.

81 Pressure

1 The sharp knife has a much smaller area of blade touching the apple, so the pressure is greater.
2 The weight of the skier is on the large area of skis, so the pressure on the snow is less and he does not sink in.
3 The force on the brake pedal creates pressure in the liquid, which is transmitted to the pistons. The large area of piston exerts a large force on to the brake pads.

82 Calculating pressure

1 a) Pressure = $20\,N / 1\,cm^2$
= $20\,N/cm^2$
b) Pressure = $20\,N / 0.01\,cm^2$
= $2000\,N/cm^2$
c) Make a much larger pressure without hurting your thumb
2 a) Pressure = $900\,N / 900\,cm^2$
= $1\,N/cm^2$
b) Pressure = $900\,N / 4500\,cm^2$
= $0.2\,N/cm^2$

83 The behaviour of light

1 Candle, lamp, star, torch.
2 a)

bright light

puppet

screen

b) Lamp moves closer, shadow gets larger as rays are spreading at a wider angle

84 Reflections

1

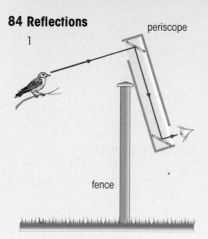

periscope

fence

2 Rays of light are scattered in all directions from the book, so it can be seen anywhere. Rays from an object reflected from the mirror are directed in a particular direction.

85 Refraction

1 When a ray of light travels from air into glass it **slows down**. This makes it change **direction**. When it comes back into air it **speeds up** and changes **direction** again. This is **refraction**.

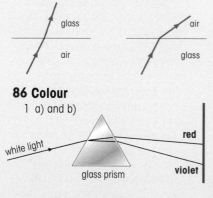

glass

air

air

glass

86 Colour

1 a) and b)

white light

glass prism

red

violet

2 Red
3 Blue
4 Black. The blue ball only reflects blue light, red light is absorbed so no colour is visible.

87 Sound vibrations

1 The strings on a guitar **vibrate** to make a sound. The thick strings will make a **low**-pitch note. If the string is tightened the pitch of the note will become **higher**. If the string is shortened the

note will become **higher**. High-pitch notes are made when the strings **vibrate** at a **high** frequency.

88 Hearing

1 Eardrum, small bones, liquid in tube, nerve changes to electrical message
2 Loud noises can damage ear drum and make the listener deaf.

89 Sound and light

1 Sound cannot travel through a vacuum but light can
2 We see the firework explode before we hear the bang

90 Movement of the Earth

1

2 In January the day is very short, the Sun rises late and sets early. As the year progresses the days get longer, until in March the day and night are each 12 hours (vernal equinox). The days continue to get longer until June (midsummer), after which the days get shorter. In September the day and night are again equal (autumnal equinox), the days continue to get shorter until the end of December when the shortest day occurs.

91 The solar system

1 Pluto
2 Mercury, it is closest to the Sun
3 There are **nine** planets in the Solar System all orbiting the **Sun**. They are held in orbit by the force of **gravity**.

92 Satellites

1 Transmit TV signals; observe the Universe; collect information about the Earth, observe the Universe
2 Gravity
3 P is closer to the Earth so will experience more force of gravity.

93 The Sun: a key energy source

1 Provides energy for plants to grow (for food); provides energy for warmth; provides energy so that it rains

2 Photosynthesis uses energy from sunlight to lock up carbon in the plant, this can later be burned as food or fuel.

3 The Sun evaporates water from the seas and via the weather system the water then falls as rain on the land.

94 Energy resources

ENERGY	renewable source	non-renewable source
directly from Sun	solar energy	
indirectly from Sun	wind, plants, waves	fossil fuels (coal, oil)
not from Sun originally	geothermal energy, tides	nuclear energy

95 Electricity generation

1 Wind, water, tides

2 Burning fossil fuels creates carbon dioxide, which contributes to global warming; we have limited supplies of fossil fuels.

3 Wind, waves, (depends on locality).

96 Storing and transferring energy

1 Do not always want energy when the Sun is shining, store the energy to use at night or on dull days

2 Distant locations from electric grid - when camping, or on a remote island

3 A lot of coal is used in a power station, it takes energy to transport the coal to the power station.

97 Temperature and heat

1 Temperature is measured in **degrees Celsius**, it tells us how **hot** something is. Heat energy is measured in **joules**, it tells us how much energy is needed to warm something up.

2 a) The tea is at a higher temperature than the room, so energy from the tea is transferred to the room. The tea cools to room temperature (may be a drop of 80°C) but the energy is spread through the whole room, so the temperature rises hardly at all.

b) Particles in the ice lolly are fixed in position, vibrating slightly. Energy from the (warmer) room is transferred to the particles, which vibrate more until the ice melts and the liquid warms to room temperature. The ice lolly has changed state and temperature, needing quite a lot of energy from the room, but the temperature of the whole room has not decreased much.

98 Energy transfer

1 a) Air is a poor conductor, so when it is trapped in the bubbles it provides a good insulating layer, but allowing light to pass into the greenhouse.

b) Warm water is less dense than cold water and rises; this is convection. A heating element warms water, which rises and this is replaced by the cold water, which can then be heated.

c) The sweat on the surface of our skin evaporates, taking away heat from the skin, which in turn cools the blood and hence the whole body.

99 Radiation

1 The black surface absorbs radiation from the Sun well, and the white car reflects the radiation, keeping it cool.

2 Energy is conducted from a gas flame to the saucepan base to the contents. Warm soup at the base is heated and rises, being replaced by cooler soup, which warms and rises. A convection current occurs within the pan. The element in an electric toaster gets hot, emitting infra red radiation, which toasts the bread.

3 The radiator warms the air around it, which causes convection currents to circulate. Radiators are often painted a light colour and so are not in fact very good radiators of energy!

100 Conservation of energy

1 a) fuel

b) warms up the surroundings

2 Use public transport or bike; wear more clothing and turn the heating down.

A

acid solutions which turn litmus red. They have pH of less than 7

adaptation how a species becomes better suited to survive in an environment

adolescence period of life prior to maturity

aerobic respiration respiration requiring free atmospheric oxygen

air sacs thin-walled divisions of the lungs

alkali solution of soluble base, which turns litmus blue and has pH of more than 7

alveoli microscopic sacs in the lungs in which exchange of gases takes place

ammeter measures the flow of electric current around a circui it is always connected in series

amnion a sac surrounding the foetus

anaemia result of having too few red blood cells

anaerobic respiration respiration via chemical changes which don't use oxygen

annelids worms that have ringed bodies, which mark the segments from which they are made (including earthworms, rag worms and leeches)

antagonistic pairs of muscles muscles which work in opposite ways such that the contraction of one is accompanied by relaxation of the other

anthropods jointed leg animals without backbones (including insects and spiders)

antibodies substances in the blood that help lead to immunity

antigen a substance, usually a protein, which when introduced into the body, stimulates the production of antibodies

atom the smallest part of an element that can exist

atomic number the atomic number (Z) of an element is the number of protons in the nucleus of its atoms

average speed speed usually changes over a journey, so we usually calculate the average speed

axis the axis of the Earth is an imaginary line from the North to the South Pole; the Earth turns around its axis each day

B

bacteria a group of microscopic organisms without nuclear membranes

ball-and-socket joint a joint which allows movement in more than one place because it is made of a ball-shaped head of bone fitting into a socket (the hip joint and the shoulder joint are examples)

base a substance that reacts with an acid to produce salt + water; bases are oxides and hydroxides of metals

biceps a muscle with two points of attachment, found in the upper arm

biomass living material

blood capillaries the smallest blood vessels in your body

blood cells cells which are carried by the blood plasma, including red cells for carrying oxygen and white cells which help defend against disease

blood system capillaries, veins and arteries which carry blood around the body

blood vessels capillaries, veins, arteries

boiling point temperature (°C) at which a liquid changes state to gas (vapour)

breathing the mechanism of getting air in and out of the lungs

breed organisms giving rise to other organisms through reproduction

bronchitis infection of the breathing tubes, called bronchi, by bacteria. Irritation of the bronchi by inhaled dust allows the bacteria to gain access

C

calcium an essential metallic element for animal and plant growth, found in dairy products; calcium is needed for bone and teeth development and for blood clotting

carbohydrate a class of compounds to which sugars, starch and cellulose belong

carbon dioxide a gas formed when all substances containing carbon are burned

cell (biol) the unit of structure and function in an organism

cell (phys) provides energy to a circuit from a chemical reaction in the cell

cell membrane membrane surrounding all animal and plant cells, which allows only certain substances to pass through

cell sap a mixture of chemicals dissolved in water which is contained in bubble-like vacuoles of plant cells

cellulose a carbohydrate that makes up the cell walls of all plants

ceramic bricks and pottery are ceramic materials, made by firing them at high temperatures in a kiln

changing state the process in which a material changes from solid to liquid, liquid to gas, or vice versa

chemical change change in which new substances are formed and which is very difficult to reverse

chemical digestion breakdown of large, insoluble food molecules into smaller, soluble ones, using digestive enzymes

chlorophyll green pigments essential to food manufacture in plants

chloroplast a structure in a cell that contains chlorophyll

cholera life-threatening disease caused by bacteria that can be carried in water

cilia tiny hair-like projections of cytoplasm

circuit a complete electric path from a cell through a lamp or other components and back to the cell

classes divisions of major groups of organisms called phyla

clot a solid mass of blood

cold-blooded animals animals which cannot keep a constant body temperature

component part of an electric circuit where energy is transferred from the electric current to something else, for example a lamp or a meter

compound formed when two or more elements are combined together chemically

concentration measurement of amount of water present in a solution

condensation change of state in which gas (vapour) becomes liquid by cooling

conduction thermal conduction is the process by which energy is transferred from a hot object to a cooler object

conductors material with low resistance, which allows an electrical current to pass

cones reproductive organs of conifers

conifers trees which have cones as reproductive organs

convection current when a liquid or gas becomes warm it expands and becomes less dense and the warm liquid or gas rises above the cooler fluid, which sinks – this flow of warm fluid is a convection current

cultivated plants that have been grown by humans in unnatural surroundings

current a flow of electric charge around a circuit, measured in amps (A)

cytoplasm the protoplasmic materials in a cell lying outside the nucleus and inside the cell membrane

D

deficiency disease a condition resulting from the lack of one or more vitamins

degrees Celsius (°C) measurement of temperature, (water boils at 100°C and freezes at 0°C)

density a measure of the amount of matter packed into a space, measured in g/cm^3 and is found by dividing mass (g) by volume (cm^3)

diffusion (biol) the spreading out of molecules in a given space from a region of greater concentration to one of less concentration

diffusion (chem) the process by which the particles of a gas spread out to completely fill its container

digestion the process during which food stuffs are chemically simplified and made soluble for absorption

digestive enzymes chemicals which break down large molecules of food to small molecules

dissolve when a solute 'disappears' into a solvent to form a solution

dynamo generates an electric current when a coil of wire spins near a magnet

E

egg a female reproductive cell

electric grid system the network used to distribute electricity from the power stations to homes, shops and factories where it is needed

electrical energy responsible for the action of our nervous system caused by movement of electrons

electromagnet a coil of wire, often wrapped around a piece of iron; the coil is connected to a switch and a power supply so it can be switched on and off

electrons small particles found in atoms. Electrons circulate around the nucleus

element single substance which cannot be broken down into anything simpler

embryo an early stage in a developing organism

emphysema a lung disease caused by breakdown of lung tissue as a result of damage due to smoking

environment the surroundings of an organism; all external forces that effect an organism's development

enzyme a protein that acts as a catalyst and so speeds by a chemical reaction without being used up

evaporation change of state in which a liquid becomes a gas (vapour); molecules near the surface of a liquid may leave the liquid to become a vapour

excretion the process by which wastes from chemical reactions are removed from cells and the body

extensor a muscle that straightens a joint

F

fallopian tubes a pair of tubes where fertilisation takes place and which lead from the ovaries to the uterus

fat a class of food which is the permanent store of energy in the body and which insulates the body from loss of heat

ferns plants which have well developed roots and stems but which do not produce flowers but produce spores on their leaves

fertilisation the fusion of two gametes

filament the very thin wire inside a light bulb is the filament, which becomes very hot and glows when an electric current passes through it

flowering plants plants which have flowers as their reproductive organs

foetus an embryo of a mammal after the main body features have formed

food classes chemicals that are the body's source of fuel or which are used to release energy from fuels, including fats, carbohydrates, protein, minerals and vitamins

force a push or pull which changes the movement or the shape of things; measured in newtons (N)

fossil fuels created over millions of years by the decay and compression of living things, particularly plants

frequency the number of waves produced each second, measured in Hertz (Hz)

friction the force between two surfaces that are rubbing against each other

fungus a plant-like organism that lacks chlorophyll and therefore obtains its food from living things or from dead and decaying things

G

gas pressure pressure exerted by the moving particles of a gas hitting the sides of the container

generators a device that uses motion to generate electricity e.g. a dynamo

genes chemicals responsible for all features that can be handed down from parents to their children

genetics the science of heredity

genus a collection of similar species

geothermal obtained from the hot rocks deep beneath the surface of the earth

gills organs modified for absorbing dissolved oxygen from the water

global warming the average temperature of the Earth has increased over the last century, this is called global warming

Glossary

glucose a carbohydrate produced by plants during photosynthesis, plants use some as an energy source and the rest is converted to starch and stored in the leaves; it is the simplest sugar and is the source of all energy in organisms; humans use it as a fuel, carried in the blood plasma

gravitational attraction the force which pulls all masses to all other masses; the bigger the mass the bigger the force

gravity the force which pulls objects to the ground; gravitational attraction acts between any two objects with mass

H

habitat a place where an organism lives naturally

haemoglobin an iron-containing protein, giving red blood cells their red colour and which carries oxygen around the body

high-storage dam water is stored in reservoirs behind a high dam and when the water is released it turns generators to produce electricity

hinge joint a joint which enables limited movement in one plane e.g. the knee joint and the elbow joint.

hormones chemicals made in glands and which are carried in the blood stream to cells where they control and regulate chemical reactions in the body

host the organism from which a parasite obtains its food

humus dead and decaying material in soil

hydraulic systems use a fluid, such as oil or water to transfer forces from one place to another

hydroelectric power electricity generated by using water to turn generators, often the water is stored in high-storage dams until the electricity is needed

I

immune system a collection of various type of cells and chemicals which enable you to defend yourself against disease

immunisation the process of making an animal resistant to infection

immunity the ability of the body to resist disease by natural or artificial means

infection the result of an invasion of harmful microbes e.g. bacteria or viruses

influenza an infectious disease of the cells lining the breathing system and caused by a virus

infrared radiation electromagnetic waves emitted by warm objects

inheritance passing down characteristics from one generation to another, for example, eye colour or hair colour

inherited a characteristic that has been passed down from past generations

insoluble when a material in a solvent will not dissolve to form a solution – a substance whose molecules cannot disperse (dissolve) in a solvent e.g. starch molecules cannot disperse in water (a solvent)

insulators a material which does not allow an electrical current to pass; it has a very high resistance

inter-particle forces forces that attract one particle to another; they are very high in a solid, less in a liquid and very low in a gas

invertebrates animals without backbones

iron a metallic element, which is very important in the makeup of haemoglobin of red blood cells

J

joint the place at which two bones meet

joules energy is measured in joules

K

kingdoms the main groups of living things, such as animals, plants, fungi and bacteria

L

lever a simple machine which helps to lift things more easily

ligament a tough strand of connective tissue that holds bones together at a joint

lignin one of the main chemicals which make up wood in plants

Glossary

liverworts primitive relatives of mosses without true leaves and are likely to have been the first type of plants to live on land

luminous something which makes light, often because it is hot, for example, the Sun, or a filament lamp

lung cancer a life-threatening disease of the lungs linked to chemicals in tobacco

lungs organs for gaseous exchange during breathing

M

magnesium a metallic element which is part of the molecule of chlorophyll

magnetic materials attract iron, and attract and repel other magnets

magnetic compass a small pointer that turns to point in the direction of a magnetic field

magnetic field the region in space around a magnet in which other magnets are affected

malaria a disease caused by a parasite that feeds on blood and which is carried by a type of mosquito

malnutrition a condition caused by not having a balanced diet

mass a measure of the amount of material in an object – it is measured in grams (g) and kilograms (kg)

measles an infectious disease caused by a virus producing a rash of red spots

mechanical digestion the breakdown of large particles of food into smaller ones by chewing

melting change of state in which a solid becomes a liquid

melting point temperature (°C) at which a solid changes its state to liquid

menstrual cycle a 28-day cycle in women during which hormones cause the release of an egg, and the development of blood vessels in the lining of the womb ready for the development of an embryo if fertilisation occurs

menstruation the periodic breakdown and discharge of the womb's lining that occurs after puberty in the absence of fertilisation

microbes organisms which can only be seen with the help of a microscope – they include bacteria, viruses, fungi and animals made of one cell

microscope an instrument that magnifies very small objects to make them visible

minerals essential classes of food which make up parts of chemicals in our bodies and which may help chemical reactions work in our bodies (e.g. iron is a mineral that makes up haemoglobin)

molecule smallest part of a compound that exists; they have two or more atoms combined together chemically

molluscs soft-bodied animals without backbones which do not have joints and which sometimes have one or more shells, for example snails and clams

moment the turning effect of a force is called the moment, measured in newton metres (Nm)

mosses primitive plants with the beginnings of leaves, stems and roots but which do not have flowers – most have to live in very moist conditions

muscles tissues made of long cells that can contract and relax

N

natural gas natural gas is a fossil fuel formed from decaying plant and animal material

natural immune system a system of cells which defend the body from disease-causing organisms

nervous system a system consisting of the brain, nerve cord and other smaller nerves which control and co-ordinate our movements and other activities

neutralisation chemical reaction between an acid and an alkali

neutron small particles found within the nucleus of an atom

newton force is measured in newtons (N)

newton metre the measurement of a moment (turning effect) - calculated by multiplying the force (N) by the distance from the pivot (m)

nicotine the substance in tobacco which causes addiction and damages the cilia lining the breathing system

nitrates chemicals found in the soil which plants need to make proteins. They are made of nitrogen and oxygen

nitrogen the gas that makes up 78% of air and is essential for the makeup of proteins

non-renewable energy sources those which can't be replaced, e.g. fossil fuels

north pole the poles of a magnet are the parts of the magnet which produce the strongest field – the north pole of the magnet is attracted to the North Pole of the Earth

nuclear membrane a thin double membrane surrounding the nucleus of a cell

nuclear reactor a power station, which uses the energy from nuclear reactions in atoms to heat water to drive turbines

nucleus the part of the cell that controls its activities

O

orbit the path of a moon around a planet or a planet around the Sun

orders divisions of classes of organisms

organ different tissues grouped together to perform a function or functions as a unit

organism a complete and entire living thing

ovaries the female reproductive organs

oviduct one of a pair of fallopian tubes in a female through which eggs travel from the ovary and in which fertilisation occurs

oxidation a chemical reaction in which oxygen is added or hydrogen is removed

oxygen the gas making up about 20% of air which is needed for the complete release of energy from glucose during aerobic respiration

oxyhaemoglobin the combination of oxygen and haemoglobin which is the form by which oxygen is carried in red blood cells to the cells of the body

P

parallel circuit an electric circuit which has branches. A break in one branch does not prevent the flow of current in another branch.

pascals pressure is measured in pascals (Pa). 1 pascal = 1 N/m^2

pathogens disease-causing microbes.

penis the male sex organ used to pass sex cells into the female vagina during sexual intercourse

periodic table table of all the elements arranged in order of their atomic number. Elements with similar chemical properties are in the same vertical group

phosphates a class of chemicals found in soils and which are essential for growth and development of plants – they consist of phosphorous and oxygen

phosphorus a metallic element essential for the makeup of phosphates

photosynthesis the process by which plant cells combine carbon dioxide and water in the presence of chlorophyll and light, to form carbohydrates and release oxygen

phyla (sing. phylum) the main sub divisions of the kingdoms of the living world, more commonly referred to as divisions

physical change change in which no new substances are formed and which is relatively easy to reverse

pitch how high or low a note is

pivot the point where a lever balances

placenta a large, thin membrane in the uterus that exchanges materials between the mother and the embryo by diffusion

plasma the liquid part of blood

platelets the smallest of the solid components of blood, which release chemicals that are needed for clotting

polio a disease of the spinal cord caused by a virus characterised by fever and sometimes paralysis

pollen the structures containing the male sex nuclei produced in the male sex organs of flowers

potassium a metallic element which is needed to keep the correct composition of body fluids, such as blood plasma

pressure the effect of a force over an area

product substance formed in a chemical reaction

prostate gland a gland located near the upper end of the urethra in a male, helping to produce semen

protein a class of food which is needed for growth and repair of tissues by the body. Rich sources are meat and fish

proton small particles found within the nucleus of an atom

protozoa animals made of a single cell

puberty the age at which the secondary sex characteristics appear

R

radiation all warm objects lose energy by emitting infrared radiation

reactants substances put together to undergo a chemical reaction

red blood cells cells carried in plasma which carry oxygen

reed relay a magnetic switch which is used to control electric circuits

refraction (of waves) happens when waves change direction due to a change in speed

relay switches (in electrical circuits) are used to control other circuits

resistance a measure of how difficult it is for an electric current to pass. Also used to describe the action of friction when an object is moving

respiration the release of energy from glucose in every living cell

respite the act of breathing in and out

ringworm a fungus which is parasitic on the skin and forms a ring-shaped blister

S

saliva a fluid secreted into the mouth by the salivary glands containing the digestive enzyme, amylase

satellite a body in orbit around a planet. Moons are natural satellites – there are many man-made satellites in orbit around the Earth

saturated solution solution containing the maximum amount of dissolved solute at a particular temperature

scurvy a disease caused by lack of vitamin C leading to bleeding gums and intestine

selective breeding the choosing of animals or plants with qualities that we find useful – they are bred to produce offspring and the best offspring are then selected to breed

semen fluid consisting of sperm and fluids from the prostate gland, and other glands found in the male's reproductive system

series circuit all the circuit components are in line and the same electric current flows through them all

sex cells the sperm of males and the eggs of females

sexual intercourse the act of inserting the male's penis into the female's vagina to discharge sperm as near to the egg as possible

skeletons structures that support and protect organs – they may occur outside or inside the body

sodium a metallic element that is needed for the correct balance of body fluids such as the plasma of the blood

solar cell uses energy from the Sun to generate an electric current

solar panels used to collect energy from the Sun, solar panels may use solar cells to generate electricity or they may use energy from the Sun to heat water in pipes passing through the panel

solubility curve graph showing the solubility of a solute in a solvent at different temperatures

solubility maximum amount of a solute (g) that will dissolve in 100g of a solvent at a particular temperature (°C)

soluble a term which refers to the ability of molecules to disperse in a solvent, for example, a salt solution is made of salt (a solute) dissolved in water (a solvent)

solute material that dissolves in the solvent to form a solution

solution mixture formed when a solute dissolves in a solvent

solvent material in which the solute dissolves to form a solution

sound wave a vibration through the air or a solid or liquid

south pole the poles of a magnet are the parts of the magnet which produce the strongest field – the south pole of the magnet is attracted to the South Pole of the Earth

space probes unmanned spacecraft sent out into space to collect data about the solar system and beyond

species a group of organisms which can breed together and produce offspring which can also breed

spectrum made when light passes through a triangular glass prism and the light is split into separate colours

speed the rate at which something moves – speed is measured in metres / second (m/s)

sperm male reproductive cells

sperm ducts tubes that carry sperm from the male reproductive organs to the tube passing through the penis called the urethra

starch the main type of carbohydrate which is stored in plants

states of matter the three states in which matter can exist are solid, liquid or gas

stomata pores regulating the passage of air and water vapour to and from leaves and stems

sub-atomic particles particles found inside atoms. The three sub-atomic particles are electrons, neutrons and protons

sugar a type of carbohydrate which is soluble in water and which is a rich source of energy, for example glucose

sulphates a class of chemicals found in the soil which are needed for plants to make proteins. They are made of sulphur and oxygen

sulphur a chemical element needed for the makeup of sulphates

survival of the fittest explains Charles Darwin's theory of evolution; meaning that only the best suited for breeding will survive to produce offspring

T

tar one of the chemicals in tobacco that causes lung cancer

tendon a strong band of connective tissue which connects a muscle to a bone

testes the male reproductive organs, which produce sperm

thermal conductor a material that allows thermal energy to be transferred through it easily

thermal insulator a material that does not allow thermal energy to be transferred through it easily

thermometer used to measure temperature – temperature is measured in degrees Celsius

tissues a collection of cells with similar functions

trachea the windpipe taking air to the bronchi

triceps a muscle with three points of attachment to the shoulder blade – it straightens the arm when it contracts

tuberculosis an infectious disease especially of the lungs caused by a bacterium – tt can be spread by milk from infected cows

turbine a machine used to turn a generator – the turbine might be driven by steam, moving water or wind

turgid describes the stiffness of plant cells due to the pressure exerted by contained water.

U

umbilical cord the link between the embryo and the placenta

urea a waste substance containing nitrogen and made in the liver

urethra a tube leading from the bladder to an external opening of the body

urine the liquid waste made in the kidney and stored in the bladder, consisting mainly of water, minerals and urea

uterus (womb) the organ in which developing embryos are nourished and protected until birth

uterus lining the inside lining of the womb which may develop into the placenta or is shed during menstruation

V

vacuoles bubble-shaped spaces scattered through the cytoplasm of a cell and containing liquid

vacuum a space with nothing in it, not even air

vagina the cavity in the female leading to the uterus

vapour a cloud of liquid particles. Steam is water vapour

variation the differences within a species caused by the environment or by inheritance

vertebrate animals with backbones

vibrate movement in which a particle shakes but does not move from place to place

vibrations a to and fro movement – vibrating objects make sounds

viruses particles that are non cellular and have no nucleus, no cytoplasm – they cannot reproduce unless they are inside living cells

vitamin C the chemical that prevents scurvy occurring. Rich sources are fresh fruits and vegetables.

vitamins chemicals which help enzymes to work in our bodies and without which we would suffer from deficiency diseases like scurvy

voice box the structure at the top of the windpipe that contains the vocal cords that vibrate to produce sound

voltage the (potential difference) between two points in a circuit measures the difference in energy carried by the electric charge passing through the circuit – voltage is measured in volts (V)

voltmeter measures the voltage between two points in a circuit – a voltmeter is connected in parallel

W

warm blooded animals animals that can keep constant body temperature, for example mammals and birds

waste materials chemicals produced during chemical reactions in the body which are not needed by the body and which could harm cells unless they leave the body

weight the force of gravity on the object. Weight is measured in newtons (N)

white blood cells colourless blood cells which have nuclei and are used for defence against disease

windpipe see trachea

X

xylem the woody tissue of plants that conducts water and dissolved minerals

Index